AF556235

THE GROWTH STRATEGIES
OF
HOTEL INDUSTRY

THE GROWTH STRATEGIES OF HOTEL INDUSTRY

By

Nancy Brown

DISCOVERY PUBLISHING HOUSE PVT. LTD.
NEW DELHI-110 002

Published by:

DISCOVERY PUBLISHING HOUSE
4383/4B, Ansari Road, Darya Ganj
New Delhi-110 002 (India)
Phone : +91-11-23279245; 23253475; 43596065
Mobile : +91 9811179893 / +91 9871656464
E-mail : discoverybooksindia@gmail.com
orderdphbooks@gmail.com
namitwasan9@gmail.com
web : www.discoverypublishinggroup.com

First Published: **2011**

Reprinted: **2026**

ISBN: 978-81-8356-924-8

The Growth Strategies of Hotel Industry

Printed at:
Infinity Imaging Systems
Delhi

PREFACE

A hotel operating business and its real estate components are closely interwoven. We have witnessed the negative impact that negligence or the mishandling of a hotel asset has on income and value. Regardless of whether you are preparing to refinance your asset, monetize equity, sell assets or boost cash flow it is beneficial to allow a real estate expert who understands the hotel industry develop a VCPS. This tool will address issues affecting a property with the goal of extracting maximum value while the hotel operator focuses on running a successful hotel.

Individuals who travel for business and vacation have many different options when choosing a hotel. For hotel owners and managers, it is necessary to promote their hotels through listings and advertisements in order to stand out in the crowd. Promotions and advertising help build brand awareness for hotels. There are a number of ways to promote hotels, and promotional materials must be unique and well-written to attract interest and elicit action.

The book has been especially written according to the requirements of the hotel industry. Our aim is to provide the whole knowledge about The Growth Strategies of Hotel Industry. We are confident that discussion made in this book will be helpful for students, Teachers and General Readers.

—Author

CONTENTS

1

INTRODUCTION

Despite the high hopes of many people on both sides, business ventures between the black investment community and the hotel industry aren't going to happen overnight.There are good intentions everywhere. Diversity is a noble endeavor for all involved, but becoming a diversified company isn't as easy as only hiring some black, American Indian or Hispanic executives or selling franchises to investors in those ethnic groups. There has to be some follow-through.

Mandalay City Hotel is an urban resort hotel that addresses the needs of value-orientated business and leisure travelers. Offering the right mix of convenience, comfort, functionality and price. Mandalay City Hotel consistently delivers quality service that is warm, responsive and professional.

The quest to become one of the top hotels in Mandalay began with the selection and recruitment of the hotel management team. Every senior manager at Mandalay City Hotel comes with operating experience from international hotels in Myanmar. To reduce the learning curve, the Mandalay City Hotel pre-opening team spent 3 months on-the-job training at an international hotel in Yangon in preparation for the pre-opening. The owner's investment in training and development will surely be one of the key factors contributing to Mandalay City Hotel's progress towards realizing its vision.

High-level officials from most hotel-franchising companies were well represented at the recent National Association of Black Hotel Owners, Operators and Developers conference in Miami Beach, Fla. It was clear that they attended to forge relationships with potential franchisees.

NABHOOD's president Andy Ingraham said that between $60 million and $70 million worth of business transactions took place during the conference. That includes franchise agreements and the acquisitions of hotels.That's a substantial sum, but could just be the beginning when it comes to minority involvement in the hotel industry.

It also was abundantly clear that the franchising representatives were there to educate and inform the black investors in attendance about the industry. For that, they deserve a round of applause. The next step for franchising companies is to provide additional educational programs for newcomers to the industry, regardless of their ethnicity.

Hotel Growth Strategies

Value Creation and Preservation

A relatively low level of hotel transactions have occurred to date and few properties are available on the market. As a result, it is difficult for many hotel owners, investors or even shareholders to continue to grow their investments through external sources with accretion as a mandate. Strategies for most growth-oriented hotel companies, whether public or private, will need to emphasize income growth from internal methods.

1. Assess Enhancement Opportunities—Those with ownership interests in hotels must be prepared to develop and encourage their operators to create sustainable income improvement solutions from all of the real estate associated with the hotel. One beneficial tool that should be utilized in maximizing the overall value of a hotel is an exhaustive Value Creation and Preservation Strategy (VCPS). This tool identifies repositioning strategies, non-traditional revenue sources, commercial and/or retail leasing opportunities, excess land use alternatives, potential benefits of capital renovation and brand repositioning, highest-and-best-use analysis and improvements in property tax burden with the overall objective of maximizing the income output of the property.

2. Review Branding and Management—The analysis would identify alternative sources for branding and/or management and the value benefits expected from each option. Implementation of the recommendations will work to improve the asset's income producing capability from hotel operations and ultimately its value. It is important to understand that some agreements tied to a hotel could be considered an encumbrance and have an adverse effect on income and value. It is always beneficial to complete a thorough due diligence on all scenarios. This component of the analysis would also benefit the passive investor or owner by having a firm knowledgeable in-management practices monitoring performance.

3. Physical Evaluation—Another factor that also plays a significant role in the long-term value prospects of a hotel is its physical condition. A deteriorating property will result in lost market share and revenue as guests seek alternative accommodation. Loss of brand affiliation is also a potential detrimental effect of a deteriorating asset. The VCPS would outline the benefits of a continuous property reinvestment plan or complete renovation. It will force hotel operators to be proactive and gauge the physical condition of the competition and fully substantiate recommendations for capital improvements. The feasibility component of a VCPS would identify the potential upside to a capital renovation providing rationale for project financing. Managing a capital renovation requires significant planning in order to minimize business disruption, reduce the potential for lost income during the renovation and deliver on time and on budget. The VCPS identifies key areas requiring planning and again rationalizes the expenditure by outlining its positive effect on income. The proper development of the renovation plan will address specific areas of expertise including architecture, engineering, legal, and construction and project management. A poorly implemented renovation can result in significant cost overruns, income erosion and destroy the desired investment returns.

4. Anticipate the Impact of New Supply—The economic life of a hotel can be adversely affected by the addition of new supply. In several cases, there have been new hotels built in markets that do not support development based on the local market operating statistics. However, some hotel developers have realized that the physical condition of the overall hotel stock within a certain market is inferior. These developers believe that a new property will steal market share from each existing hotel and on its own become successful leaving the poorest performers to suffer and possibly close or be converted to an alternative use. It is believed that this trend will continue as hotel franchisors push for brand presence in more markets. By working to develop the VCPS, a hotel owner can anticipate the effects that new supply will have on the value of their asset and devise a proactive strategy that minimizes the effect or reduces the possibility of new supply. Hotel owners need to keep in mind that the emergence of alternative forms of competition will affect the value of their hotel investments. There has been a significant rise of indirect competition in the form of furnished apartments or condominiums in major markets across Canada. This competitor has taken market share from hotels in the fairly profitable extended stay segment. The real estate in which these businesses operate is typically residential affording these entities a significant tax advantage over hotels. This is a growing industry in many markets and is establishing structure but is not easily tracked. Owners need to monitor this and other forms of non-traditional indirect competition.

5. Other Hotel Real Estate Components—Many hotels include other components that can have a significant impact on value but are often overlooked. An office or retail piece may be associated with a hotel property. These forms of real estate demand an understanding of local real estate trends in order to positively effect lease negotiations, vacancy rates and potential rental income. If an operator does not possess this expertise, it is difficult to constantly monitor activity in these areas. In addition, a highest-and-best use analysis may indicate that excess land or the overall site location would result in higher market value compared to its current use. The benefits of local market knowledge and real estate expertise can increase rental income and identify site potential to produce property value improvements.

6. Sharing the Risk - Leasing Out Components of the Operation—The opportunity to lease certain operating components within a hotel to a third party is an option that can improve a hotel's income. Some hotels have opted to lease out food and beverage operations, spas, golf courses and parking facilities to operators specializing in these disciplines. The benefit here is that the hotel now generates a more stable cash flow through lease income and the new operator will bring expertise that can improve service and product consistency. Property value can be enhanced with this arrangement since lease income is often more stable than income from operations.

7. Realty Tax Reduction—A successful property tax appeal can have a positive effect on a hotel's income. Often assessments on hospitality properties include a component of enterprise value. It is key in any assessment appeal to extract the business component from the real estate value.

The value of furniture, fixtures and equipment and management skill must be extracted to reveal only the real estate value. Assessment experts will perform research and analysis to achieve the lowest possible assessed value. This is a specialized area that is best handled by a realty company that offers professional property tax advice. A hotel operating business and its real estate components are closely interwoven. We have witnessed the negative impact that negligence or the mishandling of a hotel asset has on income and value. Regardless of whether you are preparing to refinance your asset, monetize equity, sell assets or boost cash flow it is beneficial to allow a real estate expert who understands the hotel industry develop a VCPS. This tool will address issues affecting a property with the goal of extracting maximum value while the hotel operator focuses on running a successful hotel. The Hospitality and Tourism division of Colliers International Realty Advisors has advised its clients on all aspects of value creation and preservation for their hotels. Over the last ten years it has advised on projects with an aggregate value of over $10 billion. Our clients include financial institutions, hotel owners, investors and shareholders with assets ranging from small country inns and resorts to large national portfolios.

Attendees of the NABHOOD conference were eager to learn. They have money to spend, but don't have the hotel-related knowledge to make it work without help. There can be no preconceived notions about what investors know.

Everything from explaining occupancy rates to calculating revenue per available room to detailing what a feasibility study entails are essential pieces of a puzzle that when completed will make minority investors want to keep putting their money into hotel investments.

That will take time and patience. The ultimate measurement will be in three or four years when there's an accurate count of minority-owned and operated hotels. In the meantime, franchisors have to make sure they're providing education and information to all—no matter how elementary it is or the ethnic background of a potential franchisee.

After all, in the words of every franchising salesperson that has ever been on a sales call, it doesn't do a franchisor any good if a property isn't successful.

This and That

Some rambling thoughts while wondering what ever happened to the heightened concern about safety in the lodging industry.

Cendant Corp. is considering divesting its economy-segment Knights Inn and Villager brands—the company has formed a task force that includes at least one of its brand presidents to look into the matter.

If that happens, it could actually help Cendant expand its product offering. If it chooses to divest the two brands, it could easily add a much-needed upscale brand to its portfolio. Acquiring Wyndham International is an option.

Cendant does not want to be a hotel owner, but franchising the Wyndham and Summerfield Suites brands could be a boon for the New Jersey-based company. Just as it did when it acquired timeshare player Fairfield Communities, Cendant could spin off an ownership and/or development company to sell the Wyndham assets. Or it could find a partner to buy the assets in a three-way deal with Wyndham. Either way, a Wyndham-Cendant marriage makes more sense than having Six Continents Hotels purchase Wyndham.

The American Hotel & Lodging Assn. is conducting a long-overdue study to determine if it should change its structure.

Eventually, the association will come up with a hybrid federation structure that will allow state associations to act more autonomously than they have in the past. It also will allow the AH&LA to exist more on a macro level where it won't have to rely on state associations for its members.

The day when major hotel companies can directly join the AH&LA without having to first join a state association will be a good day for the industry. At the same time, there's going to be a need for state associations to work more closely with each other and with city and regional hotel associations.

Individuals who travel for business and vacation have many different options when choosing a hotel. For hotel owners and managers, it is necessary to promote their hotels through listings and advertisements in order to stand out in the crowd. Promotions and advertising help build brand awareness for hotels. There are a number of ways to promote hotels, and promotional materials must be unique and well-written to attract interest and elicit action.

How To Promote Hotels

Contact your local yellow pages company. Place both a print and online ad in the yellow pages, the latter of which can attract out-of-town guests when they search your city for hotels. Make sure you select an ad the is comparable in size to other competitive hotels. List unique features about your hotel in the ad. Use color combinations that attract attention.

Contact travel agencies in your area and get your hotel listed with them. Consider using a link exchange promotional strategy with these agencies, where you list them on your website and they, in turn, list your hotel on their site. Go online and find large travel directories where you can list your website or advertise.

Contact some of the top hotel and travel booking sites, such as travelocity.com, expedia.com and orbitz.com. Contact the advertising department of each site and others, and get your hotel listed in the hotel links on their websites.

Join the American Hotel and Lodging Association (AH&LA). Get listed with them, but also ask them how you can get their endorsement. Start using their name and logo in your advertising after you get their permission or when you meet their requirements for membership and standards.

Go online and find a company in your area that specializes in website optimization. Have the company conduct a website analysis. Make sure you meet with them and discuss your promotional needs. Check with the local Better Business Bureau to make sure there are no complaints against the company. Have the company create an ad and link so your hotel appears on page 1 of hotel listings in your area.

Conduct satisfaction surveys with your guests. Leave space for customers to write in their comments. Use a separate form that enables a customer to provide a testimonial about their experience. Get the customer's signature. Use high customer satisfaction results and testimonials in company brochures.

Contact the welcome center and state-run rest stops in your area. Get permission to place your brochures in their display unit.

Get a list of major businesses in your area through the Direct Marketing Association. Create a sales letter that highlights the amenities and benefits of using your hotel. Mail the sales letter and a brochure to these businesses, telling them to consider your hotel for their business guests or conventions. Include a return form, if the business wants a hotel sales person to contact them.

Promote Your Hotel Website

Having a website, and not promoting it, is like buying a flashy new car and leaving it in your garage; great web site, but few people will ever see it. Some people still think that simply having a web site is enough to drive new business; wrong. The biggest problem with this thinking is that a website needs to be "found" in order to be used by its visitors; and it needs to be structured to "sell" your hotel to get reservations.

A hotel website's visibility is largely dependent upon its generic search capabilities; its ability to be found by search engines. BUT FIRST, a website needs to be compatible with search engine guidelines. Senseless flash elements, poor navigation schemes, lack of properly researched search tags, and poorly constructed text all contribute to poor search results.

Website Optimization

To be certain that your site is search and sales ready, get a comprehensive website analysis. A web site analysis consists of a page-by-page review of your site to evaluate its sales design and search ability. Your site will be analyzed for compatibility to search engine requirements, its navigation elements, sales text structure, and many other necessary web components.

Most competent site designers can provide you with an analysis of your current website. This analysis should provide you with both a subjective and objective review of the overall design, compatibility with search engines, and the effectiveness of the imbedded code or technical areas of your site. It should provide you with an easy-to-follow blueprint of suggested changes to make your site "search friendly" and "sales-ready". A site analysis, often less than $500, could be the most effective small investment you can make to improve your Internet results.

Search Engine Submissions

Ok, so you've optimized your site and you're ready to begin promoting it. Whether your site is new or recently optimized, a site launch plan, which includes search engine and directory listings, could increase its popularity and reservations production. Search engine and directory submission is a tedious process and should be left to those skilled in working with search engines.

The launch plan will, of course, include continued submission of your site to search engines and directories; setting a timetable for periodic submissions to improve visibility. There are literally hundreds of search engines and directories depending upon the sales reach of your hotel.

By attaching a data engine to your site, your web master can review the progress and results from search engines. Data-collection, from companies like Web CEO or Web Trends, takes the guess-work out of continually assessing the effectiveness of your site. Their reports can identify the most productive search referrals, popular pages on your site and other necessary marketing information, so you can be pro-active to make changes to improve your site's production.

Pay-per-click Advertising

Although there is a lot of controversy surrounding pay-per-click, it is a great way to stimulate popularity results for your site. Your site's popularity is a major factor in search engine rankings; pay-per-click can provide your site with temporary increased popularity until your site obtains good generic search ranking.

A well-researched and well-managed pay-per-click advertising program almost always provides a great return-on-investment. You can establish a monthly budget to limit your financial exposure; even very low budgets produce results. It's a great way to dominate your competition on the web. You can make your hotel dominant against the competition.

Link Structure and Strategy

Links to and from your site can provide explosive growth to the search properties of your site. In effect, a carefully developed link strategy can improve your site's visibility in ways difficult to achieve otherwise. A travel resources page can be developed to help you "borrow" popularity from the entertainment and business sites in your area.

NEVER place outgoing links on your home page; inviting visitors to leave your site too soon can be costly; links should be imbedded deeply within your site.

Create a Searchable Photo Gallery

It amazes me how many hotel web site photo galleries still contain miscellaneous images with no text definition; these photo galleries are invisible to search engines. Remember, search engines read text and ignore images when scrolling a search.

A photo gallery, complete with descriptive text, becomes a searchable page. These are some very basic ways to promote your web site; they may sound all too simple to some, but, we see way too few sites which use even these simple promotional methods. It all starts with an unprejudiced review of your site; promoting a poorly designed site, no matter how beautiful it may look, is foolish

Love Hotel

A love hotel is a type of short-stay hotel found in Japan operated primarily for the purpose of allowing couples privacy to have personal intimacy. Love hotels can usually be identified using symbols such as hearts and the offer of a room rate for a "rest" as well as for an overnight stay. The period of a "rest" varies, typically ranging from one to three hours. Cheaper daytime off-peak rates are common.

The history of love hotels can be traced back to the early Edo Period, when establishments appearing to be inns or teahouses with particular procedures for a discrete entry or even with secret tunnels for a discrete exit were built in Edo and in Kyoto. Modern love hotels developed from tea rooms used mostly by prostitutes and their clients but also by lovers. After World War II, the term *tsurekomi yado* was adopted, originally for simple lodgings run by families with a few rooms to spare. These establishments appeared first around Ueno, Tokyo in part due to demand from Occupation forces, and boomed after 1958 when legal prostitution was abolished and the trade moved underground. The introduction of the automobile in the 1960s brought with it the "motel" and further spread the concept.

The original term has since fallen into disuse within the industry itself thanks to the euphemism treadmill, and an ever-changing palette of terms is used by hotel operators keen on representing themselves as more fashionable than the competition. Alternative names include "romance hotel", "fashion hotel", "leisure hotel", "amusement hotel", "couples hotel", and "boutique hotel".

In general, reservations are not possible, leaving the hotel will forfeit access to the room, and overnight stay rates only become available after 10:00 p.m. These hotels may be used for prostitution, and while they are sometimes used by budget-travelers sharing accommodation, the practice is discouraged. Some love hotels will even refuse entry to same-sex couples (especially if they appear to be platonic backpackers) or will refuse the business of groups of three or more.

The same concept also exists in Central and South America, particularly in Guatemala, Chile and Mexico (where they are called "autohotels"), in the Dominican Republic and Colombia (where they are called "cabañas" or "motels"), and in Argentina and Uruguay, where they are often called "albergues transitorios" but are sometimes referred to as "telos" (after reversing the syllables of the word "hotel"). They are very common in Brazil and Puerto Rico, where they are simply called "motels" (the word is exclusively used for love hotels).

In the United States and Canada, certain motels in low-income urban areas (sometimes known colloquially as "no-tell motels") often serve similar functions as a Japanese love hotel. Entrances are discreet and interaction with staff is minimized, with rooms often selected from a panel of buttons and the bill settled by pneumatic tube, automatic cash machines, or a pair of hands behind a pane of frosted glass. Although cheaper hotels are often quite utilitarian, higher-end hotels may feature fanciful rooms decorated with anime characters, equipped with rotating beds, ceiling mirrors, karaoke machines, or strange lighting, or may be styled similarly to dungeons, sometimes including S&M gear.

These hotels are typically either concentrated in city districts close to stations, near highways on the city outskirts, or in industrial districts. Love hotel architecture is sometimes garish, with buildings shaped like castles, boats or UFOs and lit with neon lighting. However, some more recent love hotels are very ordinary looking buildings, distinguished mainly by having small, covered, or even no windows.

Annual Turnover

The annual turnover of the love hotel industry is more than ¥4 trillion, a figure double that of Japan's anime market. It is estimated that more than 500 million visits to love hotels take place each year, which means around 1.4 million couples, or 2% of Japan's population, visit a love hotel each day.

In recent years, the love hotel business has drawn the interest of the structured finance industry. Several transactions have been completed where the cash flows from a number of such hotels have been securitised and sold to international investors and buy-out funds. Similar establishments also exist in other East Asian countries and regions such as South Korea, Singapore, Taiwan and Hong Kong.

Promoting Hotel via Net

It has been said that the internet is the best value when it comes to hotel marketing. It has also been said that the amount of money which any hotel can invest in internet marketing is limited by its total marketing budget.

Nonetheless it is valuable to note that at times you really do not need a budget to market your hotel. This chapter gives Hoteliers four simple steps to promoting your hotel online for free or on a shoestring budget.

1. Advance your organic search listings—First and foremost Hoteliers should aim to maximize the benefits of being found by search engines such as Google and Yahoo in the organic listings and ensure the hotel website is ranking well for content that ultimately leads to increased traffic to the site.

There are several benefits of organic search listing. For example you do not pay for clicks to your hotel website, users may more readily trust organic listings and statistics indicate search tends to generate a higher conversation rate.

So how do I improve my hotel's organic search listings you may ask? Start out by identifying your target keywords that will drive traffic to your website. Gather data on performing keywords through Google's free keyword tool.

After determining which keywords are converting and appropriate for your hotel website commence optimizing your content to include these keywords. From click through to conversion you need to constantly watch the performance of your hotel website to ensure that you are being found by the widest possible variety of search engines and that the traffic is doing what it should be doing converting visitors into guests.

Next devise a link strategy which consist of identifying and targeting relevant sites for quality inbound links. Link popularity is one of the best ways to quantifiably and independently measure your website's online awareness and overall visibility. Simply put, link popularity refers to the total number of links or "votes" that a search engine has found for your website.

Did you know that you can install complete traffic tracking and reporting solution and it won't cost you a cent? Google Analytics is a free package provided by Google. It has easy to follow instructions and set-up guide.

2. Improve your website design—Give your hotel website a makeover. Today's, traveler has varied information needs for example a map and directions to your hotel and taking a glimpse inside your hotel via means of a photo gallery, virtual tour, videos and reviews. Not to forget people are not time rich these days and want a straightforward user-friendly booking process.

These days there are amazing tools and systems which can help you redesign your website or do any other work which you do not specialize in - all for pennies. One of these tools is www.Elance.com - it's a website where you can post your project requirements and dozens of professionals from all over the world will submit their bids for you to review.

You can choose the appropriate professional on the basis of reviews given by their previous customers. To redesign your entire hotel website on average it will only cost $300. Make professionals compete for your business!

3. Advertise your hotel—Have advertisers or media buying agencies ever told you that you need to spend money to make money?

This concept is not always true, for example there is a hotel website out there which offers free hotel advertising. From individual hotels to large multi-national hotel chains, HotelsCombined.com offers free accommodation listings to Hoteliers allowing you to promote your hotel to over 20 million customers worldwide each year.

HotelsCombined.com is the only site of such magnitude offering free advertising to individual properties. It seems that larger hotel chains are much faster in finding such opportunities.

4. Get into social marketing—Hoteliers get social. On the social Web, you can't buy message spread. While My Space and Facebook are attracting a lot of attention, guests are also using blogs, forums and other social media/ networks to discuss your hotel. Guest review and trip sharing websites also include Trip Advisor, Yahoo Travel and TravBuddy. What's more guests are also placing their holiday photos on Flickr.

Your goal as a Hotelier should not be to ignore social marketing but rather participate in guest discussions to influence the social Web participants who are important to you.

For example, imagine someone writes a negative forum post about your hotel. Now, imagine how much damage is going to be done if this post appears in Google when someone types your hotel name. Hoteliers should constantly monitor search engines and reply to such posts whenever possible. Once again, Google makes this easier by letting anyone to set up an alert, so you don't miss a thing!

Online Hotel Reservations

Online hotel reservations are becoming a very popular method for booking hotel rooms. Travelers can book rooms from home by using online security to protect their privacy and financial information and by using several online travel agents to compare prices and facilities at different hotels.

Prior to the Internet, travelers could write, telephone the hotel directly, or use a travel agent to make a reservation. Nowadays, online travel agents have pictures of hotels and rooms, information on prices and deals, and even information on local resorts. Many also allow reviews of the traveler to be recorded with the online travel agent.

Online hotel reservations are also helpful for making last minute travel arrangements. Hotels may drop the price of a room if some rooms are still available. There are several websites that specialize in searches for deals on rooms.

Large hotel chains typically have direct connections to the airline national distribution systems (GDS) (Sabre, Galileo, Amadeus, and Worldspan). These in turn provide hotel information directly to the hundreds of thousands of travel agents that align themselves with one of these systems. Individual hotels and small hotel chains often cannot afford the expense of these direct connections and turn to other companies to provide the connections.

Several large online travel sites are, in effect, travel agencies. These sites send the hotels' information and rates downstream to literally thousands of online travel sites, most of which act as travel agents. They can then receive commission payments from the hotels for any business booked on their websites.

Lastly, people can book directly on an individual hotel's website. An increasing number of hotels are building their own websites to allow them to market their hotels directly to consumers. Non-franchise chain hotels require a "booking engine" application to be attached to their website to permit people to book rooms in real time. One advantage of booking with the hotel directly is the use of the hotel's full cancellation policy as well as not needing a deposit in most situations.

To improve the likelihood of filling rooms, hotels tend to use several of the above systems. The content on many hotel reservation systems is becoming increasingly similar as more hotels sign up to all the sites. Companies thus have to either rely on specially negotiated rates with the hotels and hotel chains or trust in the influence of search engine rankings to draw in customers.

The ultimate service provided by these companies to the hotels and the online consumer is that they provide a single database from which all reservation sources draw immediate room availability and rates. It is very important that hotels integrate with all the supply channels so that their guests are able to make accurate online bookings.

There are many ways of making the online reservation,most of the online reservation systems use the centralized GDS system for making the reservation with the hotel directly.Examples of the GDS are Sabre, WorldSpan, Travelport,

The online hotel reservation through GDS is just the tentative reservation, means that you do not need to pay at the time of reservation, instead pay at the time of check in or check out.

Hotel Technology Next Generation

Hotel Technology Next Generation, commonly referred to as HTNG, is a global, non-profit trade association serving hotel companies and technology providers. It was founded in 2002 and is governed by a board of directors consisting of senior technology executives from hotel companies. Membership is open to companies and individuals involved with hospitality technology.

The organization's stated objective is to promote interoperability of the many technology systems used in the hotel industry, such as property management systems, point-of-sale systems, telephone systems, building automation systems, guestroom entertainment systems such as video on demand, security and access control systems, and many others.

The organization's members meet regularly in small workgroups, where hotel companies and vendors work together to design interface standards (often using XML), reference architectures, network designs, and hospitality-specific network devices. HTNG holds annual members' meetings in North America, Europe, and Asia.HTNG operates a certification program for selected specifications, administered by The Open Group.

Access Control

Access control is a system which enables an authority to control access to areas and resources in a given physical facility or computer-based information system. An access control system, within the field of physical security, is generally seen as the second layer in the security of a physical structure.

Access control is, in reality, an everyday phenomenon. A lock on a car door is essentially a form of access control. A PIN on an ATM system at a bank is another means of access control. Bouncers standing in front of a night club is perhaps a more primitive mode of access control (given the evident lack of information technology involved). The possession of access control is of prime importance when persons seek to secure important, confidential, or sensitive information and equipment.

Physical access by a person may be allowed depending on payment, authorization, etc. Also there may be one-way traffic of people. These can be enforced by personnel such as a border guard, a doorman, a ticket checker, etc., or with a device such as a turnstile. There may be fences to avoid circumventing this access control. An alternative of access control in the strict sense (physically controlling access itself) is a system of checking authorized presence, see e.g. Ticket controller (transportation). A variant is exit control, e.g. of a shop (checkout) or a country.

In physical security, the term access control refers to the practice of restricting entrance to a property, a building, or a room to authorized persons. Physical access control can be achieved by a human (a guard, bouncer, or receptionist), through mechanical means such as locks and keys, or through technological means such as access control systems like the Access control vestibule. Within these environments, physical key management may also be employed as a means of further managing and monitoring access to mechanically keyed areas or access to certain small assets.

Physical access control is a matter of who, where, and when. An access control system determines who is allowed to enter or exit, where they are allowed to exit or enter, and when they are allowed to enter or exit. Historically this was partially accomplished through keys and locks. When a door is locked only someone with a key can enter through the door depending on how the lock is configured. Mechanical locks and keys do not allow restriction of the key holder to specific times or dates. Mechanical locks and keys do not provide records of the key used on any specific door and the keys can be easily copied or transferred to an unauthorized person. When a mechanical key is lost or the key holder is no longer authorized to use the protected area, the locks must be re-keyed.

Electronic access control uses computers to solve the limitations of mechanical locks and keys. A wide range of credentials can be used to replace mechanical keys. The electronic access control system grants access based on the credential presented. When access is granted, the door is unlocked for a predetermined time and the transaction is recorded. When access is refused, the door remains locked and the attempted access is recorded. The system will also monitor the door and alarm if the door is forced open or held open too long after being unlocked.

Journey Planner

A journey planner is a specialized electronic search engine used to find the best journey between two points by some means of transport. Journey planners have been widely used in the travel industry since the 1970s by booking agents accessed through a user interface on a computer terminal, and to support call centre agents providing public transport information. With the advent of the internet, self-service browser based on-line journey planner interfaces for use by the general public have become widely available. A journey planner may be used in conjunction with ticketing and reservation systems, or just to provide schedule information.

A journey planner finds one or more suggested journeys between an origin and a destination. The origin and destination may be specified as geospatial coordinates, named topographical places (e.g. 'Timperley', 'Scunthorpe', 'Grimsby'), Points of Interest e.g. 'British Museum', or names or identifiers of points of access to public transport such as bus stops, stations, airports or ferry ports. A location finding process will typically first resolve the origin and destination into the nearest known nodes on the transport network in order to compute a journey plan over its data set of known journeys.

Journey planners for large networks typically use a search algorithm to search a graph of nodes (representing access points to the transport network) and edges (representing possible journeys between points). Different weightings such as distance, cost or accessibility may be associated with each edge.

Searches may be optimised on different criteria, for example *fastest, shortest, least changes, cheapest*. They may be constrained for example to leave or arrive at a certain time, to avoid certain waypoints, etc.

- Also known as a "Trip Planner", a Journey Planner may cover a single mode of transport, eg rail, or many transport modes for a combined journey, e.g. bus rail, air, in which case it is an Intermodal Journey Planner.
- A Road Route Planner is a journey planner specialised for road network use. Road networks

are characterised by a large number of nodes and edges which may typically be used at any time.

- A Public Transport Journey Planner (or in American English usage, a Public Transport Route planner) is specialised for journeys on Public Transport. A public transport network is characterised by a smaller graph, with services that typically run only at a particular time or at a specified frequency.

Historically a Route planner has covered just the Route, showing a path by which it is possible to travel between two points at any time; in contrast a Journey Planner has also take into account the timetable of services that run over the network only at certain times, and so the time of travel is relevant when computing a journey. However with the development of "road timetables", associating different journey times for road links at different times of day, time of travel is also relevant for road route planners.

Technology

Typically Journey Planners use an efficient in-memory representation of the network and timetable to allow the rapid searching of a large number of paths. Database queries may also be used where the number of nodes needed to compute a journey is small, and to access ancillary information relating to the journey.

A single engine may contain the entire transport network, and its schedules, or may allow the distributed computation of journeys using a distributed journey planning protocol such as JourneyWeb or Delfi Protocol.

A Journey Planner engine may be accessed by different front ends, using a Software Protocol or Application Program Interface specialised for journey queries, to provide a User Interface on different types of device.

The development of Journey Planning engines has gone hand in hand with the development of data standards for representing the stops, routes and timetables of the network, such as TransXChange, NaPTAN as well as such asTransmodel that ensure that these fit together.

History

Early journey planning planning engines were typically developed as part of the booking systems for high value transport such as air and rail, using mainframes databases and OLTP systems. Well known examples of such Computer reservations system (CRS) include Sabre, Amadeus, Galileo, and the Rail Journey Information System developed by British Rail.

As computing resources became more widely available, journey planner engines were developed to run on minicomputers, Personal computers, and mobile devices, and as internet based services accessible though Web Browsers, Mobile browsers, SMS, etc.

In the early 2000s Large scale metropolitan web planners such as Transport for London's journey planner became available. Starting in 2000 the Traveline service provided all parts of the UK with multimodal journey planning and in 2003 the Transport Direct portal was one of the first Nationwide systems, allowing comparison of travel by any mode between any two points in the country,

Many entities, including municipal government, state and federal government, and for profit companies operate web sites now offer trip planning services for large metropolitan areas, or even country-wide. For profit companies such as EasyJet, National Rail Enquiries or Deutsche Bahn typically operate sites free to people planning trips, relying on ticket sales and advertising for revenues.

As the size of the transport systems covered by journey planners has increased, protocols and algorithms for distributed journey planning have been developed, allowing the distributed computation of journeys using networks of journey planners, each computing parts of the journey for different parts of the country. The EU Spirit, JourneyWeb and the Delfi Protocol are all examples of distributed journey planning protocols. Xephos is another example of a distributed journey planning network with information populated by its user base.

Another development in the 2000s has been the addition of Real-time travel information to update the current schedules to include any delays or changes that will affect the journey plan.

In 2005 Google started developing Google Transit a journey planning engine that works in conjunction with Google Maps, using data imported in the Google Transit Data Feed Specification.

Journey planning algorithms are a classic example of problems in the field of Computational complexity theory. Real-world implementations involve a tradeoff of computational resource between accuracy and completeness of answer, and speed of the results.

National Rail

National Rail is a title used by the Association of Train Operating Companies (ATOC) as a generic term to define the passenger rail services operated in Great Britain (before the adoption of the term National Rail, "Great Britain Passenger Railway" was used). ATOC is an unincorporated association whose membership consists of the passenger train companies of Great Britain which now run the passenger services previously provided by the British Railways Board (from 1965 the Board used the title British Rail). National Rail generally does not include services that do not have a BR background; this distinction is important because National Rail services share a ticketing structure and inter-availability that do not necessarily extend to other services.

The National Rail logo was introduced by ATOC in 1999, and was used on the Great Britain public timetable for the first time in the edition valid from 26 September in that year. Rules for its use are set out in the Corporate Identity Style Guidelines published by ATOC, and available on its website.

The current edition is dated 2006, but there has been at least one previous version, dated 2000. The NR title is sometimes described as a "brand" but this, according to ATOC, is incorrect. The 2000 guidelines said: 'It has not been designed as a brand or identity, but to explain to rail travellers that there is a National Rail network and material carrying this descriptor covers all passenger Train Companies.'

National Rail should not be confused with Network Rail. National Rail is a title used to promote passenger railway services, while Network Rail is the organisation owning and managing the fixed assets (tracks, signals etc.) of the railway network.

The two networks are generally coincident where passenger services are run. Most Network Rail lines also carry freight traffic and some lines are freight only. There are some scheduled passenger services that do not run on Network Rail lines, for example Heathrow Express and The London Underground.

Train Operating Companies

About 20 privately owned Train Operating Companies, each franchised for a defined term by government, operate passenger trains on the main rail network in Great Britain. The Association of Train Operating Companies is the trade association representing the TOCs and provides several core services, including the provision of the National Rail Enquiries service.

It also runs Rail Settlement Plan (which allocates ticket revenue to the various TOCs) and Rail Staff Travel which manages the travel facilities for railway staff. It does not compile the national timetable, however, which is the joint responsibility of the Office of Rail Regulation (allocation of paths) and Network Rail (timetable production and publication).

Design and Marketing

Since the privatisation of British Rail there is no longer a single approach to design on railways in Great Britain. The look and feel of signage, liveries and marketing material is largely the preserve of the individual companies operating trains and stations.

However, National Rail continues to make use of British Rail's famous double-arrow symbol, designed by Gerald Burney of the Design Research Unit. It has been incorporated in the National Rail logotype and is also displayed on tickets, the National Rail website and other publicity. The trademark rights to the double arrow symbol remain state-owned, now being vested in the Secretary of State responsible for railway transport.

It seems likely that the continued use of the symbol immediately after privatisation had more to do with convenience than design: changing it would have made obsolete all the road signs using it to indicate railway stations. Individual operators would also have had no more right than any other private company for their "advertisement" to appear on traffic signs, whereas the double arrow (and/or the LU symbol or a PTE symbol if appropriate) was already prescribed for indicating a "railway station". However, in recent times the symbol has had a renaissance, and new stations now display it.

The lettering used in the National Rail logotype is a modified form of the typeface Sassoon Bold. Some train operating companies continue to use the former British Rail Rail Alphabet lettering to varying degrees in station signage, although its use is no longer universal; however it remains compulsory (under Railway Group Standards) for safety signage in trackside areas and is still common (although not universal) on rolling stock.

It is a common misconception that Rail Alphabet was also used for printed material, but with the exception of actual logos ("British Rail", etc.) this has never been the case. The British Rail typefaces of choice from 1965 were Helvetica and Univers, with others (particularly Frutiger) coming into use during the sectorisation period after 1983.

Today's operating companies may use what they like: some examples include Futura (Stagecoach Group), Helvetica (FirstGroup and National Express), Frutiger (Arriva Trains Wales), Bliss (CrossCountry, which is also an Arriva franchise but not branded as such), and a modified version of Precious by London Midland.

Although the companies which belong to ATOC technically compete against each other, the strapline which National Rail uses to accompany its logo is 'Britain's train companies working together'.

Other Passenger Rail Operators in Great Britain

Several conurbations in Great Britain have their own metro or tram systems, most of which are not part of National Rail. These include the London Underground, Docklands Light Railway, Blackpool Tramway, Tramlink, Glasgow Subway, Tyne and Wear Metro, Manchester Metrolink, Sheffield Supertram, Midland Metro and Nottingham Express Transit. On the other hand, the largely self-contained Merseyrail system is part of the National Rail network, and urban rail schemes around Birmingham, Cardiff, Glasgow and West Yorkshire consist entirely of National Rail services.

London Overground (LO) is a hybrid: its services are operated via a concession awarded by Transport for London, and are branded accordingly, but until 2010 all its routes used infrastructure owned by Network Rail. LO now also possess some infrastructure in its own right, following the reopening of the former East London line of London Underground as the East London Railway of London Overground. Since all the previous LO routes were operated by National Rail franchise Silverlink until November 2007, they have continued to be shown in the National Rail timetable and are still considered for some purposes to be a part of National Rail.

Two further passenger services, Heathrow Express and Eurostar, are also not part of the National Rail network despite some sharing of stations (both) and routes (Heathrow Express and Heathrow Connect only). In addition, Northern Ireland Railways was never part of British Rail, and therefore is not part of the National Rail network.

There are many privately owned or heritage railways in Great Britain, listed in the list of British heritage and private railways, which are not part of the National Rail network and mostly operate their services for heritage or pleasure purposes rather than as public transport.

Ticketing

National Rail services have a common ticketing structure inherited from British Rail. Through tickets are available between any pair of stations on the network, and can be bought from any station ticket office. Most tickets are inter-available between the services of all operators on routes appropriate to the journey being made.

A notable exception is for journeys between London and Gatwick Airport, for which, as of March 2006, three operators issue different tickets valid on their own services only. There is also a London-Gatwick ticket that is valid on all operators except Gatwick Express. Operators on some other routes offer operator-specific tickets that are cheaper than the inter-available ones.

Through tickets involving the services of Heathrow Express and London Underground are also available. Oyster pay-as-you-go can now be used on National Rail in Greater London as of 2 January 2010.

Passengers without a valid ticket boarding a train at a station where ticket-buying facilities are available are required to pay the full Open Single or Return fare. On some services penalty fares apply - a ticketless passenger may be charged the greater of £20 or twice the full single fare to the next stop. Penalty Fares can be collected only by authorised Revenue Protection Inspectors, not by ordinary Guards.

National Rail distributes a number of the technical manuals on which travel on the railways in Great Britain is based, such as the National Rail Conditions of Carriage, via their website.

Timetables

Pocket timetables for individual operators or routes are available free at staffed stations. A complete National Rail Timetable with up to 3000 pages was also available for purchase, but the last hard copy edition was published in May 2007. Complete timetables are still available in printed form from TSO (The Stationery Office) and also an independent publisher.

A digital version of the formerly printed timetable as a pdf (portable document format) file is available without charge on the Network Rail website. The National Rail Enquiries website, run by ATOC, includes a real-time journey planner, fares and live departure information.

2

THE GROWTH STRATEGIES OF AMUSEMENT INDUSTRY

The Waterpark segment of the amusement industry is growing at a faster rate — both in new facilities and in attendance — than any other segment, including amusement parks and family entertainment centers. The World Waterpark Assn. estimates 68 million people attended waterparks in the U.S. in 1999 and that figure, despite the cool and rainy weather much of the country faced this season, will be topped again in 2000.

AB reported 1999 growth of waterparks at 9%, and the WWA estimated it at 8.8%. That's compared to the 3% growth that North American amusement parks and theme parks experienced during the same period. Currently, there are an estimated 1,000 facilities that feature aquatic entertainment in the U.S. However, only 132 of them have annual attendance of more than 100,000, and only Typhoon Lagoon (1.4 million) and Blizzard Beach (1.8 million) at Walt Disney World, Lake Buena Vista, Fla., and Wet'n Wild (1.3 million) in Orlando, have attendance of more than a million.

In 1999, nearly 25 new facilities opened, and in 2000, more than a dozen opened, including two major parks, the $40 million Six Flags Hurricane Harbor, Jackson, N.J., and the $25 million Knott's Soak City USA, next to Knott's Berry Farm, Buena Park, Calif.

"I've been amazed at how strong the waterpark industry is and how fast it continues to grow, " said Kent Lemasters, president of the AmusementAquatic Management Group.

Waterpark attendance has consistently grown for several reasons, Al Turner, WWA president, pointed out. "More facilities are being built because there is a demand for waterparks, and that of course brings in new people. However, the greatest increases are coming as a result of expansion of existing facilities."

Lemasters adds that "waterparks are here to stay and we'll be seeing not only a lot of ride innovation in the future, but many changes in the look, feel, and attitudes of the waterparks themselves."

New, innovative rides have come onto the market, and while most of them are lower capacity than the traditional slides, the new rides bring a new element of water fun to the parks. "The new rides, such as the Sidewinder and the Space Bowls, are great rides to ride and they are fabulous spectator rides. People will stand and watch for hours. However, these rides don't have a lot of capacity."

But what new rides lack in capacity, they gain in marketing potential. "Put a unique ride in and it will help bring in new people, it will provide those already in the park with more choices, and it will be quite useful in the marketing of the park," Turner told AB.

Lemasters spent 15 years creating Raging Waters in San Dimas, Calif. He sold the park to Ogden Corp. in April 1999, and in early 2000, he founded his own consulting firm.

The amusement park and theme park industry in the U.S. is mature and there aren't many — if any — markets that could sustain a major new park. On the other hand, according to Lemasters, there are literally hundreds of markets still available for waterpark development.

"There are still plenty of mid-size markets out there that can support a mid-size waterpark," Lemasters told AB during the WWA Annual Convention here. "You can build a smaller, $8 million to $12 million waterpark in a smaller market with a smaller investment and still make a good go of it."

Terry Turner, (no relation to Al) VP construction maintenance and engineering at Paramount's Carowinds, and current president of the WWA, agrees with Lemasters.

"There are plenty of markets available where a waterpark could survive quite nicely," he said, pointing out Roaring Springs in Boise, Idaho, as an example. "They built a park in a community of less than 500,000 people and their annual attendance is in the 220,000 range."

Al Turner feels one reason the smaller market parks can survive now is because people know and understand what a waterpark is. "Most have seen advertisements of the big city waterparks and many have driven several hours to visit one and are usually excited when they get one in their hometown."

Al Turner also sees the mid-size waterpark as a viable half-day attraction that can easily develop its own niche. "Today, there seems to be more competition for a person's time than his money," Al Turner told AB.

Innovative new rides in a mid-size market can attract teens, an important segment that has been missing at many waterparks in the past few years. "When waterparks were mostly slides, they attracted a lot of teens," Al Turner said. "Then the teens started leaving when the family attractions, such as the rivers and the activity pools, became popular. Now, the new innovative rides are not only bringing the teens back, but are pleasing the families as well."

While waterparks and amusement parks share many challenges — such as staffing, expansion, weather and competition — waterparks have one major challenge that amusement park operators don't usually have to worry about.

In a Word, Floaters.

Two fecal-borne, diseases have come to the forefront in waterpark water quality issues. Outbreaks of E. coli and cryptosporidium have closed waterparks down during the past several years and the real problem lies with the fact that no real solution to a floater has been set in stone.

Some states say clear out the pool and close it down for 24-hours. Others say less time is OK. "Yes, that is a problem and we're working with the Centers for Disease Control on helping them set up a standardized protocol for fecal accidents," Al Turner said.

Another emerging problem involves lifeguard training. "There are several people out there questioning the basic beliefs that have been standard for more than 15 years," Al Turner said, noting that the new divergence of opinions focus on rescue techniques and scanning, the amount of time it takes to recognize a victim is in danger.

Why are waterparks doing so well? "Waterparks offer a different type of fun than amusement parks," said Terry Turner. "They are more interactive and there are more things a family can do together. Plus, water brings comfort and has a natural appeal and a healing effect."

Lemasters adds that waterparks "are just plain fun." He also points out waterparks are usually calmer and more low-key than amusement parks.

More and more theme and amusement parks are adding waterparks to their in-park line-up of activities. "If nothing more, that trend is a testimonial to the waterpark industry," Terry Turner said.

Waterpark developers are stepping outside the box and are creating parks that are truly unique. NBGS International is building a new waterpark on South Padre Island, Texas, where guests can virtually float from one attraction to another without getting out of the water (AB, Oct. 16). The Master Blaster uphill coaster will push tube riders up hills and will take passengers to the top of the various downhill attractions, eliminating the long waits on the steps.

The NBGS-designed Wild Wadi waterpark in Dubai, United Arab Emirates, was the first to use this new concept, and Jeff Henry, CEO of NBGS, said the South Padre Island project will take it "several steps further."

Al Turner sees this concept as a trend to watch in the future. "It is more fun if you don't have to get out of the water, and parks can be smaller but have higher capacities. These parks will keep you moving and will keep you wet while you wait to go down a particular slide or attraction.

"It's a good concept. Waterpark designers started out with the mentality they learned from the amusement park business, with individual attractions located in different areas of the park, each with separate lines and a gravel or cement path leading from one to another. In the future, those paths at waterparks will be water channels and while the person might have to wait " Al Turner said.

Springs in Boise, Idaho, as an example. "They built a park in a community of less than 500,000 people and their annual attendance is in the 220,000 range."

Al Turner feels one reason the smaller market parks can survive now is because people know and understand what a waterpark is. "Most have seen advertisements of the big city waterparks and many have driven several hours to visit one and are usually excited when they get one in their hometown."

Al Turner also sees the mid-size waterpark as a viable half-day attraction that can easily develop its own niche.

"Today, there seems to be more competition for a person's time than his money," Al Turner told AB.

Innovative new rides in a mid-size market can attract teens, an important segment that has been missing at many waterparks in the past few years. "When waterparks were mostly slides, they attracted a lot of teens," Al Turner said. "Then the teens started leaving when the family attractions, such as the rivers and the activity pools, became popular. Now, the new innovative rides are not only bringing the teens back, but are pleasing the families as well."

While waterparks and amusement parks share many challenges — such as staffing, expansion, weather and competition — waterparks have one major challenge that amusement park operators don't usually have to worry about.

Disney's River Country

River Country was the first water park at the Walt Disney World Resort. It opened on June 20, 1976 and ceased operations on November 2, 2001. On January 20, 2005, The Walt Disney Company announced that River Country would remain closed permanently.

Positioned on the shore of Bay Lake near Discovery Island in Lake Buena Vista, Florida, River Country was part of Disney's Fort Wilderness Resort & Campground and matched this area in its rustic wilderness theming, replete with rocks and manmade boulders (created by the same man who created Big Thunder Mountain Railroad at the Magic Kingdom).

It was described as an "old-fashioned swimming hole". The original working title before being changed was: "Pop's Willow Grove" and featured a sandy bottom and unique water filtering system using confluent water from adjacent Bay Lake, which was dammed off creating a natural-looking man-made lagoon. It was much smaller than the resort's other two water parks, Typhoon Lagoon and Blizzard Beach, with the latter nearly four times the size of River Country. Fort Wilderness Resort guests were given a discount. It was also far less busy than the other two water parks.

Magic Kingdom

Magic Kingdom is one of four theme parks at the Walt Disney World Resort located near Orlando, Florida. The first park built at the resort, Magic Kingdom opened October 1, 1971. Designed and built by WED Enterprises, the park's layout and attractions are similar to Disneyland in Anaheim, California. In 2009, the park saw an estimated 17.2 million visitors, making it the most visited theme park in the world.

Although Walt Disney himself had been highly involved in planning The Florida Project, the Walt Disney Company began construction on Magic Kingdom and the entire resort in 1967 after his death. The Magic Kingdom park was built similarly to the existing Disneyland in California. The Florida park, however, was built in a larger area and improved upon Disneyland's design.

There are several anecdotes relating to reasons for some of the features of Walt Disney World, and Magic Kingdom specifically. According to one story, Walt Disney once saw a Frontierland cowboy walking through Tomorrowland at Disneyland. He disliked how the cowboy intruded on the futuristic setting of Tomorrowland and wanted to avoid situations like this in the new park. Therefore, Magic Kingdom was built over a series of tunnels called utilidors, a blend of *utility* and *corridor*. These tunnels allow employees (aka cast members) to move through the park out of sight from guests, maintaining the illusion of the show.

Because of Florida's high water table, the tunnels could not be put underground, so they were built at the existing grade. This means that the park is actually built on the second story, giving Magic Kingdom an elevation of 107 feet (33 m). The area around the utilidors was filled in with dirt removed from the Seven Seas Lagoon, which was being constructed at the same time.

The utilidors were built in the initial construction and were not extended as the park expanded. The tunnels were only used in Magic Kingdom because of financial constraints, but they were meant to be employed in all subsequent Walt Disney World parks. Epcot's Future World and Pleasure Island each have a smaller network of utilidors.

Opening

Magic Kingdom opened as the first part of Walt Disney's planned Florida Project on October 1, 1971. It was the only theme park on the resort at the time and opened concurrently with two hotels on the property: Disney's Contemporary Resort and Disney's Polynesian Resort. The park opened with 23 attractions, three unique to the park and 20 copies of attractions at Disneyland. The Walt Disney Company promised to increase this number with more attractions like those in Disneyland as well as more unique ones. The attractions were split into six themed lands, five copies of those at Disneyland and the unique Liberty Square.

While there is no individual dedication to Magic Kingdom Park, the dedication by Roy O. Disney for the entire Walt Disney World Resort was placed within its gates.

Since opening day, Magic Kingdom has only been closed for five incidents: Hurricane Floyd, the September 11 attacks, Hurricane Frances, Hurricane Charley, and Hurricane Wilma.

Naming Confusions

Magic Kingdom has often been used as an unofficial nickname for Disneyland Park before the Walt Disney World Resort was built. The official tagline for Disneyland is *The*

Happiest Place On Earth, while the tagline for Walt Disney World's Magic Kingdom is, *The Most Magical Place On Earth.* Despite the similarities, the Florida park's tickets have always borne the official name of *Magic Kingdom.* In 1994, in order to differentiate it from Disneyland, the park was officially renamed to *Magic Kingdom Park* but is most often simply called *Magic Kingdom.* A common mistake is to add the article *the* in front of the name.

Transportation and Ticket Center

The layout of the resort places Magic Kingdom more than a mile away from its parking lot, on the opposite side of the manmade Seven Seas Lagoon. Upon arrival, guests are taken by the parking lot trams to the Transportation and Ticket Center (TTC). This facility sells tickets to the parks and provides transportation connections throughout the resort complex. It also has a small gift shop and the central lost-and-found facility for all four theme parks.

To reach Magic Kingdom, guests either use the Walt Disney World Monorail System, the Staten Island-style ferryboats, or Buses depending on the location of their hotel. The three hotels closest to Magic Kingdom, Disney's Contemporary Resort, Disney's Polynesian Resort, and Disney's Grand Floridian Resort and Spa use either the ferry or monorail system to travel to Magic Kingdom.

Guests staying at Disney's Wilderness Lodge and Disney's Fort Wilderness Campground can also ride a dedicated ferry boat to the Magic Kingdom docks. The other hotels take the buses to travel to this specific park. The three ferries are clad in different trim colors and are named for past Disney executives: the General Joe Potter (blue), the Richard F. Irvine (red) and the Admiral Joe Fowler (green).

The main monorail loop has two lanes. The outer lane is a direct nonstop loop between the TTC and Magic Kingdom. The inner loop has additional stops at Disney's

Contemporary Resort, Disney's Polynesian Resort and Disney's Grand Floridian Resort & Spa. Epcot is accessible by a spur monorail line that was added upon that park's opening in 1982.

LANDS OF THE MAGIC KINGDOM

The park map lists 46 attractions in six themed "lands." Designed like a wheel with the hub in front of Cinderella Castle, pathways spoke out across the 107 acres (0.43 km^2) of the park and lead to these seven lands. The Walt Disney World Railroad runs along the perimeter of the park and makes stops at Main Street, U.S.A. and Frontierland.

Main Street, U.S.A.

Instead of being a replica of a small Midwestern American town, Main Street at Magic Kingdom features some stylistic influences from around the country. Taking its inspiration from New England to Missouri, this design is most noticeable in the four corners area in the middle of Main Street, where each of the four corner buildings represents a different architectural style. There is also no Opera House on Magic Kingdom's Main Street as there is at Disneyland; instead, there is the Exposition Hall.

Main Street is lined with shops selling merchandise and food. The decor is early-20th century small-town America, inspired by Walt Disney's childhood and the film Lady and the Tramp. City Hall contains the Guest Relations lobby, where cast members provide information and assistance. A working barber shop gives haircuts for a fee. The Emporium carries a wide variety of Disney souvenirs such as plush toys, collectible pins and Mickey-ear hats. Tony's Town Square and the Plaza Restaurant are table service restaurants. Casey's Corner is at the end of Main Street and sells traditional American ballpark fare including hot dogs and fries. The Main Street Confectionary sells sweets priced by their weight, such as candied apples, crisped rice treats, chocolates, cookies and fudge.

Most windows on Main Street bear the name of people who were influential at Walt Disney World or other Disney parks. An example of a classic Main Street, U.S.A. attraction is the Walt Disney World Railroad, which transports guest throughout the park, making stops at Frontierland and Mickey's Toontown Fair.

In the distance beyond the end of Main Street stands Cinderella Castle. Though only 189 feet (55m) tall, it benefits from a technique known as forced perspective. The (fake) second stories of all the buildings along Main Street are shorter than the first stories, and the third stories are even shorter than the second, and the top windows of the castle are much smaller than they appear. The resulting visual effect is that the buildings appear to be larger and taller than they really are.

Symbolically, Main Street, U.S.A. represents the park's "opening credits". Guests pass under the train station (the opening curtain), then view the names of key personnel along the windows of the buildings' upper floors. Many windows bear the name of a fictional business, such as "Seven Summits Expeditions, Frank G. Wells President", with each representing a tribute to significant people connected to the Disney company and the development of Walt Disney World Resort.

The park contains two additional tributes: the *Partners* statue of Walt Disney and Mickey Mouse in front of Cinderella Castle and the *Sharing the Magic* statue of Roy O. Disney sitting with Minnie Mouse in the Town Square section of Main Street, U.S.A. Both were sculpted by veteran Imagineer Blaine Gibson.

Adventureland

Adventureland represents the mystery of exploring foreign lands. It is themed to resemble the remote jungles in

Africa, Asia, the Middle East, South America and the South Pacific, with an extension resembling a Caribbean town square. It contains classic rides such as Pirates of the Caribbean and Jungle Cruise.

Frontierland

Frontierland is where guests can relive the Wild West – from cowboys and Indians, to exploring the mysteries of the Rivers of America. Frontierland contains classic attractions such as Big Thunder Mountain Railroad, Splash Mountain, and the Country Bear Jamboree.

Liberty Square

This area of the park is based on an American Revolutionary town. The Magic Kingdom's Rivers of America hosts the Liberty Belle riverboat. Liberty Square is home to the Haunted Mansion and the Hall of Presidents.

Fantasyland

In the words of Walt Disney: "Fantasyland is dedicated to the young at heart and to those who believe that when you wish upon a star, your dreams come true." Fantasyland is themed in a medieval-faire/carnival style.

Attractions include "it's a small world", Peter Pan's Flight, Dumbo the Flying Elephant, The Many Adventures of Winnie the Pooh, Mickey's PhilharMagic, Snow White's Scary Adventures, Prince Charming Regal Carrousel, and Mad Tea Party.

Expansion

The land is currently undergoing a large expansion and renovation. "The New Fantasyland will be constructed in phases with most new experiences open by 2013."

Recent conceptual artwork for the expansion shows several new additions and changes. Included is a new dark ride themed to Disney's 1989 film The Little Mermaid (also opening at Disney California Adventure) and an area themed to Disney's 1991 film Beauty and the Beast featuring The Beast's Castle with a new dining experience, Gaston's tavern, and Belle's cottage.

Snow White's Scary Adventures will be removed and an area themed to Disney's 1937 film Snow White and the Seven Dwarfs will be built. It will feature Snow White's cottage and The Seven Dwarfs mine train roller coaster ride. Princess Fairytale Hall, a new Disney Princess meet and greet will be established where Snow White's Scary Adventures currently exists.

Mickey's Toontown Fair closed permanently in February of 2011 in order to make way for the expansion. Some elements of Mickey's Toontown Fair will be demolished and others will be re-themed to a new Storybook Circus area. An expanded Dumbo the Flying Elephant ride will be built with an interactive queue. The Barnstormer at Goofy's Wiseacre Farm will be re-themed, "featuring Goofy as The Great Goofini."

Tomorrowland

In the words of Walt Disney: "Tomorrow can be a wonderful age. Our scientists today are opening the doors of the Space Age to achievements that will benefit our children and generations to come. The Tomorrowland attractions have been designed to give you an opportunity to participate in adventures that are a living blueprint of our future."

Tomorrowland is themed to be an intergalactic city. Classic attractions include Space Mountain and the Tomorrowland Speedway.

Mickey's Toontown Fair

An expansion of the land created as Mickey's Birthdayland, and later Mickey's Starland, this area was home to attractions such as Mickey's Country House, Minnie's Country House, Goofy's Barnstormer, and Donald's Boat.

This land closed permanently on February 12, 2011 to make way for the expansion of Fantasyland. The Walt Disney World Railroad station in Mickey's Toontown Fair will be closed for the duration of the construction.

Director Jon Favreau and the studio Walt Disney Pictures plan to produce and release a film concerning a family at Disneyland who finds the theme park characters and attractions coming to life.

Favreau, who said "the Disney iconography was probably the first set of archetypes that I was exposed to" and that Disney movies and attractions "made a deep impression on me as a child", noted that, "When I first heard about the ['Magic Kingdom' film] project, I was on my way to visit Disneyland with my family. I took notes and had no problem filling a book with all the ideas that this concept offered, even on first blush."

Marc Abraham and Eric Newman of Strike Entertainment are scheduled to produce the film. Writer-producer Ronald D. Moore had previously written an original script for the project, which the studio eventually declined to use, saying Favreau and a new screenwriter will develop a new script.

Growth of Theme Parks

The theme park has several historical antecedents, including the ride-based amusement parks of early 20th century America and the garden parks of Europe.

The birth of the modern theme park, however, is commonly recognized as occurring with the opening of Disneyland about 30 years ago.

Economics Research Associates (ERA) has completed many assignments for the Walt Disney Company over the years, and, since Disneyland, theme parks have multiplied throughout the world. And they all bear the following primary characteristics:

1. They have a family appeal;
2. They contain one or more themed environments;
3. They have some form of "ambient entertainment." That is, strolling, musicians, performers, costumed characters and the like, who performs for "free";
4. They have a high investment level per unit of ride or show capacity;
5. They have high standards of service and maintenance and cleanliness;
6. They contain enough activities (entertainment content) to create an average visitor length of stay of typically 5 to 7 hours; and finally,
7. They will usually, but not always, have a pay-one-price admission policy.

Recently, there have been variations from the formula. These include theme parks oriented around one theme or toward one market. This includes aquatic parks and children's parks. A second departure from the traditional theme park is indoor theme parks combined with retail shopping centers. The largest examples of these are West Edmonton Mall in Canada, Lotte World in Seoul and Mall of America in Minneapolis.

State of the Industry

The theme park industry has witnessed a fairly rapid international expansion in recent years. Growth has been focused mostly in Europe and Japan. It is instructive to compare industry development in the U.S. with where other world markets stand.

The U.S. industry has had about a 30-year growth to maturity. This was characterized by an inception period pioneered by Disney in the late 50s and early 60s, rapid growth period through the 70s, and maturity in the 80s. Europe and North Asia are currently in the rapid growth phase of their theme park industries. The developing countries are in the inception period. While the U.S. experience can not be directly translated to foreign markets, we can be reasonably assured that Europe, and North Asia will continue to have fairly strong growth over the next 10 years or so, and it will be 5 years or more before we see any significant growth in the developing countries.

Europe

Europe has a number of existing parks. The industry is spread throughout western Europe with a large concentration of attractions in Germany, France, the Benelux countries, and the United Kingdom. Expansion of the industry into southern Europe is now taking place, with several planned or implemented projects in Spain, Italy, Turkey, and Greece. There are also a number of proposed projects in North Africa and the Middle East.

Currently, the European theme park industry consists of 19 major attractions with annual attendance of over 1 million, and some 45 moderate-scale attractions with attendance between 500,000 and 1 million. Europe's parks generate annual attendance of about 70 million persons, and revenues of around $1.5 billion. The European industry is about 1/3 the size of the U.S. industry in terms of revenues.

The European market is changing, of course, with the recent opening of the EuroDisney project.

The watchwords for Europe are anticipation, repositioning, expansion and consolidation.

1. Anticipation—Wherever Disney theme parks enter new markets there are significant structural changes to the indigenous theme park industries. In the U.S., Disney's first attraction, Disneyland, founded the industry. In Florida,

Disney's attraction converted an unknown swamp into America's premier tourist destination and attraction market, and in Japan, Tokyo Disneyland spurred growth of the Japanese theme park industry. We believe Disney will have a significant impact on the attractions' industry in France and Europe. This impact will be in six key areas:

1. EuroDisney will expand the overall European theme park industry and focus the industry in Paris by creation of a multi-park destination attraction complex.
2. Disney will educate the market as to the theme park product, the quality of the theme park experience, and the value of the pay-one-price admission for a day of quality entertainment.
3. Disney will provide price leadership in the market. This will allow others to price up to Disney levels.
4. EuroDisney will create marketing awareness. Disney's well established and creative marketing programs will create awareness in the market and also enlighten competitors relative to the use of effective marketing techniques.
5. EuroDisney will improve management expertise in the European theme park business. EDL will train and create a labor pool of experienced theme park managers which will in the future help to enhance the performance of the European theme park business as a whole.

Finally, EDL will create the need for proper product positioning to complement Disney in the market area. A variety of target marketing and positioning strategies have proven successful elsewhere in markets shared with Disney parks.

2. Repositioning—Many of the European parks have been expanding and repositioning with a renewed emphasis on reinvestment and marketing. Many European attractions have undertaken major expansion programs increasing ride and show capacity and expanding visitor services such as restaurants and merchandise areas (areas where European parks have traditionally lagged behind the U.S.). Major expansion programs have occurred at Alton Towers in England, De Efteling, in Holland, Gardaland in Italy, Parc Asterix in France, Walibi in Belgium, and other European attractions. Several European parks have repositioned themselves in the marketplace. In the past, the parks relied on steady repeat business from the immediate resident market. This market responded to the attraction's low admission prices, picnic areas, and relatively passive environments which offered a quasi-public park experience. Through recent reinvestment programs, parks have repositioned themselves as more active and commercial attractions with higher admission prices, and drawing from somewhat larger markets.

3. Expansion—The European theme park industry has also been marked by new development activity in recent years. In the last four years, new attraction development has been focused primarily in France. EuroDisney opened in 1992 but was preceded (perhaps unwisely) by four other new attractions:

- Asterix,
- The Smurf Park,
- Mirapolis, and
- Zygofolis.

Disney has yet to be well accepted by the French market although it is doing quite well with tourists. The other new French parks have struggled financially, due to flaws in design, development, and management. Two (Mirapolis and Zygofolis) have gone bankrupt and significantly damaged the enthusiasm of investors and lenders. Busch is proceeding with its park in Tarragona, Spain and several other new projects are proposed in Southern Europe. Legoland is also expanding to several new key markets.

4. Consolidation—A final trend in the European theme park business is the consolidation of the industry into key ownership groups. This occurs in industries as they mature and has also been a trend in the U.S. In Europe, several attraction acquisitions have begun this process. In 1990, Madame Tussauds purchased Alton Towers (Madame Tussauds also owns several smaller attractions on the Continent and the Rock Circus attraction in London). The Walibi organization purchased The Smurf Park (now called Walibi Smurf), increasing their theme park industry holdings to four parks. Finally, Accor, France's largest hotel operator, acquired a controlling interest in Parc Asterix. With European unification and the continuing maturation of the European theme park industry, this trend will continue. It is too early to determine trends for the Soviet Union and Eastern Europe but a number of schemes have surfaced including theme parks oriented toward increasing tourism based foreign exchange. Because of the rapid changes in these markets, we may have to wait some time before we see any significant development in the amusement and theme park industry. However, we should keep our eye on them. Winston Churchill may have put it this way "Never in the history of mankind have so many been so un-amused for so long."

North Asia

Asia is the world's next leading international theme park market. It includes a mature industry in Japan, strong growth in Korea, strong performance in Hong Kong, underserved markets in Taiwan, and a rapidly changing China.

A substantial amusement park industry has been established in Japan since the recovery from the post-war period. A variety of themed attractions and numerous amusement parks are located throughout the country. the growth of this business has been assisted by the presence of major amusement ride manufacturers in Japan.

There are strong concentrations of amusement and theme parks in the Kanto region around Tokyo and the Kansai region near Osaka and Kobe. These are the two main urban areas in Japan and they both have huge population bases which support a variety of attractions. A third concentration, now in the formative stages, is on the southern island of Kyushu. The Kyushu area is developing as a resort destination area which includes several parks and attractions, including Harmonyland.

Tokyo Disneyland, which opened in 1983, brought the large-scale theme park product to Japan, and since that time, several large projects have been built including the $630 million Puroland in Tama, and Nippon Space World in Kyushu. Several other large projects are currently being planned or underway.

The Japanese industry at present has about 29 large parks with annual attendance over 1 million persons, and 30 moderate-scale parks with attendance between 500,000 persons and 1 million persons. As a whole, the Japanese industry generates about 75 million attendees and about $1.5 billion in annual revenues. This places the Japanese industry at about 30 percent of the U.S. industry in terms of revenues. On a revenue per capita basis, however, they are reasonably close.

The watchwords for Asia are selective growth and short term retrenchment.

1. Growth—For the last five to seven years there has been a strong interest in theme park development in Japan and Korea. Much of this was catalyzed by the success of Tokyo Disneyland. Other factors driving Japanese interests in theme parks have been the high level of discretionary income available for entertainment, and a heightened national interest in leisure. Also, the Japanese government, until very recently, has provided strong incentives for leisure development. There are several-large scale theme park projects under consideration at this time. These include a second-gate attraction at Tokyo Disneyland, which may be a movie studio park or the Disney Sea attraction originally planned for Long Beach, California, a major sea life park in the Awaji area near Osaka, a large-scale theme park proposed for a large landfill area in Kobe, MCA's Universal Studios Japan project, expansion of Yongin Farmland in Korea, expansion of Ocean Park, Hong Kong, several proposed projects in Taiwan, and a push by China to encourage theme park investment. There are also numerous other projects being discussed.

2. **Retrenchment**—In the last year or so, there has been a retrenchment of the theme park industry in Japan. In the late 1980s, major Japanese corporations entered this industry with gusto. Unfortunately, their efforts were met in many cases with design, operating, and financial difficulties at some of the major projects which were opened. Several poorly performing projects which have been financial drains on the major corporations which have developed them, have created an air of caution in Japan about the theme park business. This combined with economic ills being faced in different segments of the country's economy have slowed down the growth of the theme park industry as the Japanese reassess what makes this industry work, and what the model for Japan should be.

Developing World

Developing countries are concerned with many economic and social development issues. Some see tourism as a major force for economic improvement and look to themed attractions as part of the tourism product. There is also a growing resident market that has the income necessary to afford attractions.

It is instructive to look at the world's population distribution. Right now, 78 percent of the world's 5.4 billion people, or 4.2 billion people, live in developing countries. By the year 2010, 82 percent of the world's population will live in these countries. Even if 20 percent of these people are income-qualified for a theme park product, that is a market approaching 1 billion people! And many of these economies, particularly in Asia, are expanding and have rising income levels.

It will be some time before the developing countries have major theme or amusement park industries, but some countries should be seeing development activity in the near term. Countries to keep an eye on are Brazil, Mexico, India, Thailand, the Middle East, and the Southeast Asian growth triangle of Singapore, Malaysia and Indonesia.

North America

The U.S. theme park industry is by far the largest in the world. There are approximately 40 large-scale parks with annual attendance of over 1 million, and approximately 55 moderate-scale parks with attendance between 500,000 and 1 million.

Annual attendance at these attractions totals 159 million persons with revenues of $4.5 billion. The U.S. industry dominates the world, in scale, product innovation, marketing savvy, and operating knowledge.

The U.S. is a mature industry. Growth has been at a compounded annual rate of about 3 percent over the last 10 years. About ½ of this growth has come from the addition of new parks and not from attendance increases in existing parks. Per capita expenditures have slightly exceeded the rate of inflation, reflecting admission price increases and strong growth in merchandise sales and games revenues. When we combine attendance growth with per capita expenditure increases, we see an annual revenue growth of about 9 percent over the last 10 years.

The watchwords for the U.S. industry are: maturation, consolidation, diversification, and destination tourism.

1. **Maturation**—The majority of U.S. markets capable of supporting large-scale, outdoor theme parks already have them. It is unlikely that a significant number of major regional theme parks will be developed in the future. Growth in this industry has stabilized, and there should not be any huge fluctuations in attendance or development activity. However, there are opportunities for adjusting product to suit changing markets and to effectively compete with other entertainment for consumers' leisure time and expenditures.

2. **Consolidation**—Typical of a maturing industry, there have been numerous changes in theme park ownership over the last several years. This indicates a strong consolidation trend. Much of the control of the industry is now focused into a few multi-park operating companies: Disney, Time Warner/Six Flags, Paramount/KECO, Anheuser Busch and MCA-Universal.

Three major corporations have left the industry (Taft Broadcasting, Marriott Corporation, and Harcourt Brace Javonavich). In 1984, Taft's entertainment group, King's Entertainment Company (known as KECO) for a $167.5 million in a leverage buyout transaction, KECO now owns five parks and manages a sixth in Australia. They have recently been acquired by Paramount.

The Marriott Corporation sold its two parks to divest themselves from the industry.

One was in Santa Clara and is now owned by KECO, and the other was in the Chicago area and is now owned by Six Flags.

HBJ, previous owners of the Sea World parks, sold all of their parks to Busch, which already owned two parks. Busch's theme park holdings now total seven with a planned attraction in Spain.

The seven Six Flags parks have been sold as a group several times and are now owned by Time/Warner. Four of the Six Flags parks started by independent operators.

Disney continues to increase their ownership in the industry by building more attractions. Within the last several years they have opened three attractions: the Disney/MGM Studio Tour, Typhoon Lagoon, and Pleasure Island. Disney has also announced plans for additional attractions in Anaheim on Disneyland-adjacent property.

3. Diversification—The U.S. theme park industry is diversifying into new smaller-scale targeted products for "niche" markets which may not be covered by the large-scale theme parks.

ERA feels that this trend is being driven by market opportunities like those which drove expansion of the theme park industry several decades ago. The theme park development boom in the 1970s represented a massive, heavily capitalized response to the need to provide baby boomers with family entertainment. Theme parks fit into the urban fabric of America by being located next to large, built-in metropolitan markets, and on relatively inexpensive land.

The 80s witnessed a narrowing of market and product focus with the smaller investment waterparks. This was the first major diversification of the industry. Waterparks appealed to a more narrow market, usually teens and young families, and were suitable for smaller secondary markets.

The new entertainment attractions of the 90s represent a furthering diversification. These attractions narrow the niche appeal even more with smaller capital investment and an appeal usually to very specific market groups such as children, teens, young singles, etc. Many of these attractions begin to tap the "baby boomlet", and respond to the need to regenerate under-performing suburban real estate properties by locating in shopping centers.

Examples of the new entertainment attractions include the family entertainment centers being developed in malls, the expansion of the outdoor family recreation and mini-golf attractions, entertainment centers combined with urban mixed use projects, sports bars, themed restaurants, children's attractions, mini-aquariums, and a host of others.

Diversification should continue as entrepreneurs attempt to seek out untapped entertainment markets.

4. Destination Tourism—Within the last 10 years, the only major parks developed in the U.S. have been destination market parks focusing on the tourist markets of the sunbelt states of Florida, and Texas. these attractions have included Disney's EPCOT Center, Disney's MGM Studio Theme Park, Universal Studios - Florida, and Sea World Texas in San Antonio. One exception was Marine World Africa U.S.A., which was relocated from one area of the San Francisco Bay region to another. Additionally, the major planned attractions: Disney's new California attraction, Fiesta Texas in San Antonio, and the possible Columbia Pictures attraction in California, will all be destination in nature. Theme park development in the U.S. has changed from selling a 7-hour experience to a 7-day experience. Disney, of course is the pioneer in this thinking. Developers have realized the incredible economic value created by the impact of a tourism oriented theme park on surrounding complementary properties such as hotels, resorts, and shopping centers.

THEME PARKS AND TOURISM

Turning now to the relationships of theme parks to tourism. These relationships are complex and highly dependent on the park's scale, quality. and uniqueness.

Typically, residents (from within 1.5 to 2 hours) will account for 80 percent of traditional theme park visitation. Even the tourist visitors are often in the area for other reasons (such as visiting friends and relatives). Thus, just having a theme park does not automatically insure an influx of tourism. Rather, to impact destination tourism, a theme park must:

Be unique, a "must see" destination.

This can be accomplished through character development (Mickey and his friends), architectural form, natural features, special events and programming (Opryland) or a combination thereof.

Have large scale and a critical mass of attractions.

Investment levels to impact international tourism generally must exceed U.S. $150 million.

Combine high technology with human scale and quality service.

Investments in the thrill hardware must be combined with a high level of service from the "hosts and hostesses" so that a unique local culture and friendly human contact is balanced to the high technology.

Encourage overnight stays.

The principal economic benefits of tourism come when overnight stays are generated. Day visitors or tourists who stay with friends and relatives generate only 20 percent of the economic impact of tourists staying in hotels and motels ($50 versus $250 per day). Thus, in designing a theme park for tourism, a multiple attraction destination (with experiences that can occupy two or three days) is more likely to have the desired impact.

Have complementary destination activities.

Tourist-oriented theme parks should be part of a mix of recreation and leisure activities. A true tourist destination would also have supporting recreation uses such as high quality hotels, convention and conference facilities, resorts, recreational shopping and dining experiences, and sports activities including golf, tennis, and water-related activities, and excursions into nearby local tourism areas.

Support media (TV) coverage and exposure.

Like most other things in life, future theme parks must be designed for television. The use of theme parks and resorts as backdrops for variety programs, celebrity games, sports competition, and convention/conference broadcasting is increasing rapidly and the resultant TV exposure is very important in creating awareness in tourism markets.

Given that these criteria are part of the theme park/tourist destination program, the results can be dramatic and provide a sustaining economic base. For example, at Walt Disney World tourism increased from 2.8 million visitors in 1970 to over 35 million by 1992. The increase in the number of air visitors alone was 20 million. This increase in visitation (particularly overnight visitation) spurred the development of over 50,000 hotel rooms and resulted in the direct employment of over 250,000 persons. Quite a success story for what was once only a mosquito infested swamp bought for an average price of $200 per acre. Smaller scale attractions, such as Polynesian Cultural Center in Hawaii, have also built a steady business of nearly a million visitor a year through strong penetration of the tourism market.

Developing Trends

As we moved toward the year 2000, how will theme parks evolve as a component of international tourism. They will not blindly follow the U.S. model, but evolve new forms of attractions where tourism is a more important source of market support. From our perspective in analyzing development trends and proposed new parks, we see the following changes:

Themed to country/region

New parks will have stronger theming tied to the country or local region. Theme parks are increasingly becoming a symbol and showcase for regional pride, culture, and technological achievement. The danger her, of course, is that by being too serious about "cultural" tourism the parks can cease to be fun. We have to constantly counsel our clients that a theme park's prime objective is entertainment. This is the "sugar" that makes the learning and culture pill work.

Part of Larger Mixed-use Destination Projects

In the urban/suburban context, we now see theme parks and large scale attractions being designed into regional and specialty shopping complexes, mixed-use waterfront developments, and even some multi-use office buildings. In more rural settings, additional components often include destination resorts, bungalow parks, shopping/restaurant villages, and special events centers/trade expositions.

Greater Visitor Participation and Interaction

New attractions are being designed to provide greater participant control and encourage interplay between the visitor and his environment. This is a natural outgrowth of both available technology and the demonstrated appeal of such involvement at places like the San Francisco Exploratorium. New thrill rides are being offered where the rider can individually control the experience and intensity of the ride. Future thematic concepts will be based more on participative activities (sports, music) that relate to the audience rather than comic book characterizations.

Use of Simulation Experiences and Virtual Reality

Perhaps one of the most exciting areas of development is in the area of simulation. Advances in technology have allowed attractions designers to realistically duplicate virtually any natural or special effects experience. By combining extremely high quality visual imagery with seats that are programmed to move with the action, visitors can realistically enjoy experiences that were previously unavailable in a theme park environment. The first highly popular example of this technology is the Star Tours attraction at Disneyland. However, new simulation presentation include river rafting in New Zealand, runaway sports cars in the Italian Alps, and intergalactic space races. These simulations are produced for a fraction of the cost of traditional attractions. The technology is also more flexible (you can change the experience by simply changing the software (film) rather them creating a new attraction), and more land efficient (a 45-seat simulator needs only about 300 square meters). A major challenge, however, will be to have the technology breakthrough and still maintain the thrill and spontaneity of perceived personal risk and group interaction.

Greater Water Orientation

A greater use of water related activities, attractions and landscaping is occurring in theme park design as well as in nearly all forms of real estate development. Several parks (Ocean Park, Hong Kong; Dreamland, Australia; Walibi, Belgium) combine an active water park with more traditional themed rides and amusements. Performance parks such as Sea World are still popular but future expansion will be limited by restrictions on capturing and displaying aquatic mammals. We see a continuing acceptance of new, high technology aquariums using acrylic tunnel concepts which combine a scuba diver's view of the undersea world with a ride experience. Some of these will be developed in the open ocean.

Design For All-weather Operation/artificial Environments

New theme parks are designed to have more covered attractions as well as climate controlled walkways and rest areas. This allows for shorter amortization of high capital investment and fixed cost components. New theme parks are being designed with a greater degree of weather protection in order to enable a longer operating season and longer operating hours per day.

When one looks ahead at the larger number of tourists who are expected to travel to new destinations (particularly within the Asia - Pacific region), there will be increasing pressure on sensitive environmental and social resources at the destination. A new role for theme parks is emerging. By their nature, they are designed to handle large numbers of people within a controlled space and with manageable impacts.

In the future, they will embody a greater educational function to introduce, interpret, and sensitize the overseas tourist to the environment and to the host community and its values. They can become a new gateway for host country tourism. Rather than being viewed as a stand alone attraction, theme parks will become part of a balanced leisure product and tourism system that contributes to the economic development, employment, and resource preservation of an entire region.

Growth Strategy of Disneyland

The concept for Disneyland began when Walt Disney was visiting Griffith Park with his daughters Diane and Sharon. While watching them ride the merry-go-round, he came up with the idea of a place where adults and their children could go and have fun together. His dream lay dormant for many years. Walt Disney also may have been influenced by his father's memories of the World's Columbian Exposition of 1893 in Chicago.

Walt Disney came up with the concept of Disneyland after visiting various amusement parks with his daughters in the 1930s and 1940s. He initially envisioned building a tourist attraction adjacent to his studios in Burbank to entertain fans who wished to visit; however, he soon realized that the proposed site was too small. After hiring a consultant to help determine an appropriate site for his project, Walt bought a 160-acre (65 ha) site near Anaheim in 1953.

Construction began in 1954 and the park was unveiled during a special televised press event on July 17, 1955.

Since its opening, Disneyland has undergone a number of expansions and renovations, including the addition of New Orleans Square in 1966, Bear Country (now Critter Country) in 1972, and Mickey's Toontown in 1993. Disney California Adventure Park was built on the site of Disneyland's original parking lot and opened in 2001.

Disneyland Park is a theme park located in Anaheim, California, owned and operated by the Walt Disney Parks and Resorts division of The Walt Disney Company. Known as Disneyland when it opened on July 18, 1955, and still colloquially known by that name, it is the only theme park to be designed and built under the direct supervision of Walt Disney. In 1998, the theme park was re-branded "Disneyland Park" to distinguish it from the larger Disneyland Resort complex.

Disneyland has a larger cumulative attendance than any other theme park in the world, with close to 600 million guests since it opened. In 2009, 15.9 million people visited the park, making it the second most visited park in the world that calendar year.

The Midway Plaisance there included a set of attractions representing various countries from around the world and others representing various periods of man; it also included many rides including the first Ferris wheel, a "sky" ride, a passenger train that circled the perimeter, and a Wild West Show. Another likely influence was Benton Harbor, Michigan's nationally famous House of David's Eden Springs Park. Walt Disney visited the park and ultimately bought one of the older miniature trains originally used there; the colony had the largest miniature railway setup in the world at the time.

While many people wrote letters to Walt Disney about visiting the Disney Studio, he realized that a functional movie studio had little to offer to the visiting fans. This began to foster ideas of building a site near his Burbank studios for tourists to visit. His ideas then evolved to a small play park with a boat ride and other themed areas. Disney's initial concept, his "Mickey Mouse Park", started with an 8-acre (3.2 ha) plot across Riverside Drive. Disney started to visit other parks for inspiration and ideas, including Tivoli Gardens, Greenfield Village, The Efteling, Tilburg, Playland, and Children's Fairyland. He started his designers working on concepts, but these would grow into a project much larger than could be contained in 8 acres (3.2 ha).

Disney hired a consultant, Harrison Price from Stanford Research Institute, to gauge the proper area to locate the theme park based on the area's potential growth. With the report from Price, Disney acquired 160 acres (65 ha) of orange groves and walnut trees in Anaheim, southeast of Los Angeles in neighboring Orange County.

File

Difficulties in obtaining funding prompted Disney to investigate new methods of fundraising. He decided to use television, and created a show named *Disneyland* which was broadcast on the then-fledgling ABC television network. In return, the network agreed to help finance the new park. For the first five years of its operation, Disneyland was owned by Disneyland, Inc., which was jointly owned by Walt Disney Productions, Walt Disney, Western Publishing and ABC. In 1960 Walt Disney Productions purchased ABC's share (it had earlier bought out Western Publishing and Walt Disney). In addition, many of the shops on Main Street, U.S.A. were owned and operated by other companies who rented space from Disney.

Construction began on July 16, 1954 and cost $17 million to complete. The park was opened one year and one day later. U.S. Route 101 (later Interstate 5) was under construction at the same time just to the north of the site; in preparation for the traffic Disneyland was expected to bring, two more lanes were added to the freeway before the park was finished.

July, 1955: Dedication Day and Opening Day

Disneyland Park was opened to the public on July 18, 1955 with only 20 attractions. A special "International Press Preview" event was held on Sunday, July 17, 1955, which was only open to invited guests and the media. The Special Sunday events, including the dedication, were televised nationwide and anchored by three of Walt Disney's friends from Hollywood: Art Linkletter, Bob Cummings, and Ronald Reagan. ABC broadcast the event live on its network.

The event did not go smoothly. The park was overcrowded as the by-invitation-only affair was plagued with counterfeit tickets. Only 11,000 people were expected to show up, but a staggering 28,154 was the eventual population. Movie stars and other famous figures scheduled to come every two hours showed up all at once. All major roads nearby were empty. The temperature was an unusually high 101 °F (38 °C), and a plumbers' strike left many of the park's drinking fountains dry. Disney was given a choice of having working fountains or running toilets and he chose the latter.

This generated negative publicity since Pepsi sponsored the park's opening; disappointed guests believed the inoperable fountains were a cynical way to sell soda. The asphalt that had been poured just that morning was so soft that ladies' high-heeled shoes sank into it. Vendors ran out of food. A gas leak in Fantasyland caused Adventureland, Frontierland, and Fantasyland to close for the afternoon. Some parents were seen throwing their children over the shoulders of crowds to get them onto rides such as the King Arthur Carrousel.

The park got such bad press for the "International Press Preview" that Walt Disney invited attendees back for a private "second day" to experience Disneyland properly. In later years Disney and his 1955 executives referred to July 17, 1955 as "Black Sunday". Today, cast members wear pin badges on July 17 in celebration of the park's anniversary, stating how many years it has been since the 1955 opening. But for the first decade or so, Disney officially stated that opening day was on July 18, 1955 and celebrated the 18th as its Anniversary. For example, a 1967 Disneyland press release referred to July 17, 1955, as "Dedication Day" and not "Opening Day."

On Opening Day, Monday July 18, crowds started to gather in line as early as 2 a.m., and the first person to buy a ticket and enter the park was David MacPherson with admission ticket number 2, as Roy O. Disney arranged to pre-purchase ticket number 1 from Curtis Lineberry, the manager of admissions. Walt Disney had an official photo taken with two children, Christine Vess Watkins (age 5) and Michael Schwartner (7); the photo of the three carries an inaccurate caption identifying the children as the first two guests of Disneyland. Watkins and Schwartner both received lifetime passes to Disneyland that day, and MacPherson was awarded one shortly thereafter, which was later expanded to every single Disney-owned park in the world. Approximately 50,000 guests attended the Monday Opening day.

The Early Years

In September 1959, Soviet Premier Nikita Khrushchev spent thirteen days in the United States. On his visit Khrushchev had two requests: to visit Disneyland and to meet John Wayne, Hollywood's top box-office draw. Due to the Cold War tension and security concerns, he was famously denied an excursion to Disneyland. The Shah of Iran and Empress Farah were invited to Disneyland by Walt Disney in early 1960s. The video of the Shah and Disney riding the Matterhorn roller coaster is available on YouTube.

As late as 1963, civil rights activists were still pressuring the park to start hiring black employees, according to Neal Gabler's biography of Walt Disney.

Park Becomes Resort

In the late 1990s, work began to expand on the one-park, one-hotel property. Disneyland Park, the Disneyland Hotel and the site of the original parking lot as well as acquired surrounding properties were earmarked to become part of a greater vacation resort development. The new components of this resort were to be another theme park, Disney's California Adventure Park; a shopping, dining and entertainment complex, Downtown Disney; a remodeled Disneyland Hotel; Disney's Grand Californian Hotel & Spa; and the acquisition of the Pan Pacific Hotel (later to be remodeled and renamed Disney's Paradise Pier Hotel). Because the existing parking lot (south of Disneyland) was built upon by these projects, the six-level, 10,250-space "Mickey and Friends" parking structure was constructed in the northwest corner of the property. At the time of its completion in 2000, it was the largest parking structure in the United States.

The park's management team during the mid-1990s was a source of controversy among Disneyland fans and employees. In an effort to boost profits, various changes began by then-executives Cynthia Harriss and Paul Pressler. While their actions provided a short-term increase in shareholder returns, they drew widespread criticism from employees and guests alike for the lack of foresight. With the retail background of Harriss and Pressler, Disneyland's focus gradually shifted from attractions to merchandising. Outside consultants McKinsey & Company were also brought in to help streamline operations, which resulted in many changes and cutbacks. After nearly a decade of deferred maintenance, Walt Disney's original theme park was showing visible signs of neglect. Fans of the park decried the perceived decline in customer value and park quality and rallied for the dismissal of the management team.

Disneyland in the 21st Century

Matt Ouimet, formerly the president of the Disney Cruise Line, was promoted to assume leadership of the Disneyland Resort in late 2003. Shortly afterward, he selected Greg Emmer as Senior Vice President of Operations. Emmer is a long-time Disney cast member who had worked at Disneyland in his youth prior to moving to Florida and held multiple executive leadership positions at the Walt Disney World Resort. Ouimet quickly set about reversing certain trends, especially with regards to cosmetic maintenance and a return to the original infrastructure maintenance schedule, in hopes of restoring the safety record of the past. Much like Walt Disney himself, Ouimet and Emmer could often be seen walking the park during business hours with members of their respective staff. They wore cast member name badges, stood in line for attractions and welcomed comments from guests.

In July 2006, Matt Ouimet announced that he would be leaving The Walt Disney Company to become president of Starwood Hotels & Resorts Worldwide. Soon after this announcement, Ed Grier, executive managing director of Walt Disney Attractions Japan, was named president of the Disneyland Resort. Greg Emmer retired from his job on February 8, 2008. In October 2009, Ed Grier announced his retirement, and was replaced by George Kalogridis as the new President of the Disneyland Resort.

Lands of Disneyland

Disneyland has eight themed areas or "lands" that host various shops, restaurants, live entertainment, and attractions. A ninth area (albeit defunct) is Holidayland, a picnic ground which operated between 1957 and 1961 and is often referred to as the "lost" land of Disneyland.

Main Street, U.S.A.

Main Street, U.S.A. is patterned after a typical Midwest town of the early 20th century. Walt Disney derived inspiration from his boyhood town of Marceline, Missouri and worked closely with designers and architects to develop the Main Street appeal. It is the first area guests see when they enter the park (if not entering by monorail), and is how guests reach Central Plaza. At the center of The Magic Kingdom and immediately North of Central Plaza stands Sleeping Beauty Castle, which provides entrance to Fantasyland by way of a drawbridge across a moat. Adventureland, Frontierland, and Tomorrowland are arrayed on both sides of the castle.

" For those of us who remember the carefree time it recreates, Main Street will bring back happy memories. For younger visitors, it is an adventure in turning back the calendar to the days of grandfather's youth. "

— ***Walt E. Disney***

Main Street, U.S.A. is reminiscent of the Victorian period of America with the train station, town square, movie theater, city hall, firehouse complete with a steam-powered pump engine, emporium, shops, arcades, double-decker bus, horse-drawn streetcar, jitneys and other bits of memorabilia. Main Street is also home to the Disney Art Gallery and the Opera House which showcases *Great Moments with Mr. Lincoln* a show featuring an Audio-Animatronic version of the president. There are many specialty stores on Main Street including: a candy store, jewelry and watch shop, a silhouette station, a store that sells Disney collectable items created by various artists, and a hat shop where you have the option of creating your own ear hat along with a personalized embrodiery. At the far end of Main Street, U.S.A. is Sleeping

Beauty Castle, and the Central Plaza (also known as the Hub), which is a portal to most of the themed lands. Several lands are not directly connected to the Central Plaza—namely, New Orleans Square, Critter Country and Mickey's Toontown.

The design of Main Street, U.S.A. uses the technique of forced perspective to create an illusion of height. Buildings along Main Street are built at 3/4 scale on the first level, then 5/8 on the second story, and 1/2 scale on the third—reducing the scale by 1/8 each level up.

Adventureland

Adventureland is designed to recreate the feel of an exotic tropical place in a far-off region of the world. "To create a land that would make this dream reality", said Walt Disney, "we pictured ourselves far from civilization, in the remote jungles of Asia and Africa." Attractions include opening day's Jungle Cruise, the "Temple of the Forbidden Eye" in Indiana Jones Adventure, and Tarzan's Treehouse, which is a conversion of the earlier *Swiss Family Robinson Tree House* from the Walt Disney film, Swiss Family Robinson. Walt Disney's Enchanted Tiki Room which is located at the entrance to Adventureland is the first feature attraction to employ Audio-Animatronics, a computer synchronization of sound and robotics.

New Orleans Square

New Orleans Square is a themed land based on 19th-century New Orleans. It was opened to the public on July 24, 1966. Despite its age, it is still very popular with Disneyland guests, being home to some of the park's most popular attractions: Pirates of the Caribbean and the Haunted Mansion, including nighttime entertainment in Fantasmic!. Also included are the Mark Twain Riverboat, the Sailing Ship Columbia, and Pirate's Lair on Tom Sawyer Island. The above-mentioned attractions are sometimes mistakenly placed as Frontierland attractions.

Frontierland

Frontierland recreates the setting of pioneer days along the American frontier. According to Walt Disney, "All of us have cause to be proud of our country's history, shaped by the pioneering spirit of our forefathers. Our adventures are designed to give you the feeling of having lived, even for a short while, during our country's pioneer days." Frontierland is home to the Pinewood Indians band of animatronic Native Americans, who live on the banks of the Rivers of America. Entertainment and attractions include Big Thunder Mountain Railroad and Frontierland Shootin' Exposition. Frontierland is also home to the Golden Horseshoe Saloon, an Old West-style show palace. Currently the comedic troupe "Billy Hill and the Hillbillies" entertains guests at the Golden Horseshoe.

Critter Country

Critter Country opened in 1972 as "Bear Country", and was renamed in 1988. Formerly the area was home to Indian Village, where indigenous tribespeople demonstrated their dances and other customs. Today, the main draw of the area is Splash Mountain, a log-flume journey inspired by the Uncle Remus stories of Joel Chandler Harris and the animated segments of Disney's Academy Award-winning 1946 film, Song of the South. In 2003, a dark ride called The Many Adventures of Winnie the Pooh replaced the Country Bear Jamboree, which closed in 2001. The Country Bear Jamboree presented shows featuring singing bear characters that were visualized through Disney's electronically controlled and mechanically animated puppets, known as Audio-Animatronics.

Fantasyland

Fantasyland is the area of Disneyland of which Walt Disney said, "What youngster has not dreamed of flying with Peter Pan over moonlit London, or tumbling into Alice's nonsensical Wonderland? In Fantasyland, these classic stories of everyone's youth have become realities for youngsters – of all ages – to participate in." Fantasyland was originally styled in a medieval European fairground fashion, but its 1983 refurbishment turned it into a Bavarian village.

Attractions include several dark rides, the King Arthur Carrousel, and various family attractions. Sleeping Beauty's Castle once again features a walk-through story telling of Briar Rose's adventure as Sleeping Beauty. Opened in 1959, changed in 1972, then closed in 1992 for reasons of security and the new installation of pneumatic ram firework shell mortars for "Believe, There's Magic in the Stars". The walkthrough reopened 2008 and it features new renditions and methods of storytelling and the restored work of Eyvind Earle (not Mary Blair).

Many Fantasyland attractions close approximately one hour before fireworks are scheduled to begin.

Fantasyland has the most fiber optics in the park; more than half of them are in Peter Pan's Flight.

Mickey's Toontown

Mickey's Toontown opened in 1993 and was partly inspired by the fictional Los Angeles suburb of Toontown in The Walt Disney Studios' 1988 release Who Framed Roger Rabbit. Mickey's Toontown is based on a 1930s cartoon aesthetic and is home to Disney's most popular cartoon characters. Toontown features two main attractions: Gadget's Go Coaster and Roger Rabbit's Car Toon Spin. The "city" is also home to cartoon character's houses such as the house of Mickey Mouse, Minnie Mouse and Goofy, as well as Donald Duck's boat.

Tomorrowland

During the 1955 inauguration Walt Disney dedicated Tomorrowland with these words: "Tomorrow can be a wonderful age. Our scientists today are opening the doors of the Space Age to achievements that will benefit our children and generations to come. The Tomorrowland attractions have been designed to give you an opportunity to participate in adventures that are a living blueprint of our future." Disneyland producer Ward Kimball had rocket scientists Wernher von Braun, Willy Ley, and Heinz Haber serve as technical consultants during the original design of Tomorrowland. Initial attractions included Rocket to the Moon, Astro-Jets and Autopia; later, the first incarnation of the Submarine Voyage was added. The area underwent a major transformation in 1967 to become *New Tomorrowland,* and then again in 1998 when its focus was changed to present a "retro-future" theme reminiscent of the illustrations of Jules Verne.

Current attractions include Space Mountain, Innoventions, Captain EO Tribute, Autopia, the Disneyland Monorail Tomorrowland Station, the Astro Orbitor and Buzz Lightyear Astro Blasters. Finding Nemo Submarine Voyage opened on June 11, 2007, resurrecting the original Submarine Voyage which closed in 1998. Star Tours was closed in July 2010, to be replaced with a brand new attraction called "Star Tours: The Adventures Continue" in 2011.

Theatrical Terminology

Disneyland staff use theatrical terminology. This is to emphasize that a visit to the park is intended to be similar to witnessing a performance. For example, visitors are referred to as "guests" and park employees as "cast members". "On stage" refers to any area of the resort that is open to guests. "Backstage" refers to any area of the resort that is closed to guests. A crowd is referred to as an "audience". "Costume" is the attire that cast members who perform the day-to-day operations of the park must wear. Terms such as "uniform" are not used. "Show" is the resort's presentation to its guests, such as the color and façades of buildings, placement of rides and attractions, costumes to match the themed lands.

When signing credit card receipts for souvenirs or food, guests are asked for their "autograph". "Stage managers" are responsible for overseeing the operation of the different areas of the park. Cast members who are in charge of a specific team are called "leads," as in a film or theater "lead role". In the earlier years of the park, the offices where administrative work took place were referred to as "production offices". "Production schedulers" build employee work schedules to meet the necessary workload, while "stage schedulers" handle day-to-day changes in that work schedule (such as a change in park hours, necessitating a change in everybody's shifts).

Each cast member's job is called a "role". When working in their roles, cast members must follow a "script". This is not a traditional play script, but more of a strict code of conduct and approved, themed phraseology that cast members may use when at work. Park employees are often reminded that "no" and "I don't know" are not a part of a cast member's script.

Backstage areas include closed areas of attraction, store, and restaurant buildings, as well as outdoor service areas located behind such buildings. Although some areas of the park, particularly New Orleans Square, have underground operations and storage areas, there is no park-wide network of subterranean tunnels, such as Walt Disney World's utilidors.

There are several points of entry from outside the park to the backstage areas: Ball Gate (from Ball Road), T.D.A. Gate (adjacent to the Team Disney Anaheim building), Harbor Pointe (from Harbor Boulevard), and Winston Gate (from Disneyland Drive).

Berm Road encircles the park from Firehouse Gate (behind the Main Street Fire Station) to Egghouse Gate (adjacent to the Disneyland Opera House). The road is so called because it generally follows outside the path of Disneyland's berm. A stretch of the road, wedged between

Tomorrowland and Harbor Boulevard, is called Schumacher Road. It has two narrow lanes and runs underneath the Monorail track. There are also two railroad bridges that cross Berm Road: one behind City Hall and the other behind Tomorrowland.

Major buildings backstage include the Frank Gehry-designed Team Disney Anaheim, where most of the division's administration currently works, as well as the Old Administration Building, behind Tomorrowland. The Old Administration Building additionally houses the Grand Canyon and Primeval World dioramas visible on the Disneyland Railroad.

The northwest corner of the park is home to most of the park's maintenance facilities, including:

- Company vehicle services, including Parking Lot trams and Main Street Vehicles
- Scrap yard, where the Resort's garbage and recyclables are sorted for collection
- Circle D Corral, where the Resort's horses and other animals are stabled
- Parade float storage and maintenance
- Distribution center for all Resort merchandise
- Ride vehicle service areas
- Paint shop
- Sign shop

Backstage also refers to parts of show buildings that are normally not seen by guests. Backstage areas are generally off-limits to park guests. This prevents guests from seeing the industrial areas that violate the "magic" of on-stage and keeps them safe from the potentially dangerous machinery. Cast members can also find some solace while they work or rest, as backstage offers alternate routes between the park's various areas.

Many attractions are housed in large, soundstage-like buildings, some of which are partially or completely disguised by external theming. Generally, these buildings are painted a dull green color in areas not seen by guests; ostensibly, this choice has been made to help disguise the buildings among the foliage and make them less visually obtrusive. Walt Disney Imagineering has termed this color, "Go Away Green." Most of them have off-white flat roofs that support HVAC units and footpaths for cast members. Inside are the rides, as well as hidden walkways, service areas, control rooms, and other behind-the-scenes operations.

Photography is forbidden in these areas, both inside and outside, although some photos have found their way to a variety of web sites. Guests who attempt to explore backstage are warned and often escorted from the property. The boundary between on and off-stage is demarcated at every access point. Everything within guest view when a door or gateway is open is also considered on stage. It is from this point, that characters start playing their part. That way, when the door is open, guests will not accidentally see a person out of character backstage.

Various amenities exist for Cast Members backstage when they are on breaks, or before and after their scheduled shifts. A number of cafeterias, now run by Sodexo, offer discounted meals throughout the day. These include Inn Between (behind the Plaza Inn), Eat Ticket (near the Team Disney Anaheim building behind Mickey's Toontown), and Westsider Grill (located approximately behind New Orleans Square). Partners Federal Credit Union, the credit union for employees of The Walt Disney Company in Orange County, provides nearly 20 ATMs backstage for cast member use and maintains an express branch at the Team Disney Anaheim building.

Transportation

Walt Disney had a longtime interest in transportation, and trains in particular. Disney's passion for the "iron horse" led to him building a miniature live steam backyard railroad—the "Carolwood Pacific Railroad"—on the grounds of his Holmby Hills estate. Throughout all the iterations of Disneyland during the seventeen or so years when Disney was conceiving it, one element remained constant: a train encircling the park. The primary designer for the park transportation vehicles was Bob Gurr who gave himself the title of Director of Special Vehicle Design in 1954.

Disneyland Railroad

Encircling Disneyland and providing a grand circle tour is the Disneyland Railroad (DRR), a short-line railway consisting of five oil-fired and steam-powered locomotives, in addition to three passenger trains and one passenger-carrying freight train. Originally known as the Disneyland and Santa Fe Railroad, the DRR was presented by the Atchison, Topeka and Santa Fe Railway until 1974. From 1955 to 1974, the Santa Fe Rail Pass was able to be used in lieu of a Disneyland "D" coupon.

With a three-foot gauge, the most common narrow gauge measurement used in North America, the track runs in a continuous loop around The Magic Kingdom through each of its realms. Each turn-of-the-19th-Century train departs Main Street Station on an excursion that includes scheduled station stops at: New Orleans Square Station; Toontown Depot; and Tomorrowland Station. The Grand Circle Tour then concludes with a visit to the "Grand Canyon/Primeval World" dioramas before returning passengers to Main Street, U.S.A.

Disneyland Monorail System

One of Disneyland's signature attractions is its monorail service, which opened in Tomorrowland in 1959 as the first daily-operating monorail train system in the Western Hemisphere. The monorail guideway has remained almost exactly the same since 1961, aside from small alterations while Indiana Jones Adventure was being built. Five generations of monorail trains have been used in the park, since their lightweight construction means they wear out quickly. The most recent operating generation, the Mark VII, was installed in 2008. The monorail shuttles visitors between two stations, one inside the park in Tomorrowland and one in Downtown Disney. It follows a 2.5 mile (4 km) long route designed to show the park from above. Currently, the Mark VII is running with the colors red, blue and orange.

The monorail was originally built with one station in Tomorrowland. Its track was extended and a second station opened at the Disneyland Hotel in 1961. With the creation of Downtown Disney in 2001, the new destination is Downtown Disney, instead of the Disneyland Hotel. The physical location of the monorail station did not change, but the original station building was demolished as part of the hotel downsizing, and the new station is now separated from the hotel by several Downtown Disney buildings, including ESPN Zone and the Rainforest Café.

Main Street Vehicles

All vehicles that are found on Main Street were designed to accurately reflect turn-of-the-century vehicles, including a double-decker bus, a horse-drawn streetcar, a fire engine, and an automobile. They are available for one-way rides along Main Street, U.S.A. The horseless carriages are modeled after cars built in 1903. They are two-cylinder, four-horsepower (3 kW) engines with manual transmission and steering. Walt Disney used to drive the fire engine around the park before it opened, on most mornings. It has also been used to host celebrity guests and used in the parades.

Disneyland Helipad

From the late 1950s to 1968 Los Angeles Airways provided regularly scheduled helicopter passenger service between Disneyland and Los Angeles International Airport (LAX) and other cities in the area. The helicopters initially operated from Anaheim/Disneyland Heliport, located behind Tomorrowland.

Service later moved, in 1960, to a new heliport north of the Disneyland Hotel. Arriving guests were transported to the Disneyland Hotel via tram. The service ended after two fatal crashes in 1968: The crash in Paramount, California, on May 22, 1968 killed 23 (the worst helicopter accident in aviation history at that time). The second crash in Compton, California on August 14, 1968, killed 21.

Live Entertainment

In addition to the attractions, Disneyland provides live entertainment throughout the park. Most of the mentioned entertainment is not offered daily, but only on selected days of the week, or selected periods of the year.

Characters

Many Disney characters can be found throughout the park, greeting visitors, interacting with children, and posing for photos. Some characters have specific areas where they are scheduled to appear, but can be found wandering as well.

Periodically through recent decades (and most recently during the summers of 2005 and 2006), Mickey Mouse would climb the Matterhorn attraction several times a day with the support of Minnie, Goofy, and other performers. Other mountain climbers could also be seen on the Matterhorn from time to time. As of March 2007, Mickey and his "toon" friends no longer climb the Matterhorn but the climbing program continues.

Daily Ceremonies

Every evening at dusk, there is a military-style flag retreat to lower the Flag of the United States for the day, performed by a detail of the Disneyland Security Personnel.

The ceremony usually is held between 4 and 5 pm, depending on the entertainment being offered on Main Street, USA, to prevent conflicts with crowds and music. Disney does report the time the Flag Retreat is scheduled on its Times Guide, offered at the entrance turnstiles and other locations.

THE DISNEYLAND BAND

The Disneyland Band, which has been part of the park since its opening, plays the role of the Town Band on Main Street, U.S.A. It also breaks out into smaller groups like the Main Street Strawhatters, the Hook and Ladder Co., and the Pearly Band in Fantasyland.

Fantasmic!

Fantasmic!, which debuted in 1992, is a popular multimedia nighttime show on the Rivers of America. The star Mickey Mouse summons the characters and spirit of beloved Disney cartoons and uses the power of imagination to defeat the evil villains that try to turn his dream into a nightmare. The presentation is made at the Laffite's Tavern end of Pirate's Lair at Tom Sawyer Island and uses the Rivers of America as part of the stage. It uses Frontierland and New Orleans Square as the spectator arena.

It consists of synchronized lighting and special effects, with floating barges, the Mark Twain Riverboat, the Sailing Ship Columbia, fountains, lasers, fireworks, thirty-foot-tall "mist screens" upon which animated scenes are projected, and an automated 45-foot fire-breathing dragon.

Fireworks

Elaborate fireworks shows synchronized with Disney songs and often have appearances from Tinker Bell or Dumbo, flying in the sky above Sleeping Beauty Castle. Since 2000, presentations have become more elaborate, featuring new pyrotechnics, launch techniques and story lines. In 2004,

Disneyland introduced a new air launch pyrotechnics system, reducing ground level smoke and noise and decreasing negative environmental impacts. At the time the technology debuted, Disney announced it would donate the patents to a non-profit organization for use throughout the industry.

During the holiday season, there is a special fireworks presentation called *Believe... In Holiday Magic*, which has been running since 2000, except for a hiatus in 2005 during the park's 50th anniversary celebration.

Scheduling of fireworks shows depends on the time of year. During the slower off-season periods, the fireworks are only offered on weekends. During the busier times, Disney offers additional nights. The park offers fireworks nightly during its busy periods, which include Easter/Spring Break, Summer and Christmas time. Disneyland spends about $41,000 per night on the fireworks show.

The show is normally offered at 8:45 PM if the park is scheduled to close at 10 pm or later, but shows have started as early as 5:45 pm. A major consideration is weather/winds, especially at higher elevations, which can force the cancellation of the show. The park will usually wait an additional 15 minutes or so to see if the winds die down. Shows, with a few minor exceptions, such as July 4 and New Year's Eve, must finish by 10 pm due to the conditions of the permit issued by the City of Anaheim.

The Golden Horseshoe Revue

The Golden Horseshoe Saloon offers a live stage show with a Old West feel. The Golden Horseshoe Revue was an American frontier-themed vaudeville show starring Sluefoot Sue and Pecos Bill. It ran until the mid-1980s, when it was replaced by a similar show starring Lily Langtree (or Miss Lily) and Sam the Bartender. Most recently, Billy Hill and the Hillbillies have played their guitars and banjos in a bluegrass-and-comedy show.

Additionally, in front of the Golden Horsehose Saloon, The Laughing Stock Co. enacts small humorous skits with an Old West theme.

Parades

Disneyland has featured a number of different parades traveling down the park's central Main Street - Fantasyland corridor. There have been daytime and nighttime parades that celebrated Disney films or seasonal holidays with characters, music, and large floats. One of the most popular parades was the Main Street Electrical Parade, which now resides at the Magic Kingdom at Walt Disney World in Lake Buena Vista, Florida.

From May 5, 2005 through November 7, 2008, as part of the Disneyland's 50th Anniversary, Walt Disney's Parade of Dreams was presented, celebrating several of the classic Disney stories including The Lion King, The Little Mermaid, Alice in Wonderland, and Pinocchio.

In 2009, Walt Disney's Parade of Dreams was replaced by *Celebrate! A Street Party*, which premiered on March 27, 2009. Disney does not call *Celebrate! A Street Party* a parade, but rather a "street event." During the Christmas season, Disneyland presents "A Christmas Fantasy" Parade.

On July 30, 2010, the Disney Parks Blog announced that a new parade, *Mickey's Soundsational Parade*, would arrive in Disneyland in 2011. The parade is set to debut on May 27, 2011.

3

THE GROWTH STRATEGIES OF BARS AND NIGHTCLUBS

Undoubdetly, opening a new restaurant whether it's your first or fortieth entails risk, usually lots of it. It's estimated that of the half million or so restaurants in the U.S. around 10 to 15 percent are forced to close each year. Most of these failures are restaurants that have been open fewer than three years. It takes lots of planning, capital, hard work, perseverance, and a little luck doesn't hurt either, to launch a new restaurant that hits the mark and becomes a financial success. There are many factors that can increase a new restaurant's chances for success in the areas of planning, location, market analysis, concept, menu, financial feasibility, staffing, operating systems and more. We are focused on bring content in a variety of formats to these areas with the objective of providing you with resources that will enhance your ability to better plan the opening process, evaluate the financial feasibility, make more informed decisions and go into the development process with tools to stay organized and on track with your plan.

Bar and Alcoholic Drinks

A bar is an establishment that serves alcoholic drinks — beer, wine, liquor, and cocktails — for consumption on the premises. Bars provide stools or chairs that are placed at tables or counters for their patrons. Some bars have entertainment on a stage, such as a live band, comedians, go-go dancers, or strippers.

Types of bars range from dive bars to elegant places of entertainment for the elite. Many bars have a happy hour to encourage off-peak patronage. Bars that fill to capacity sometimes implement a cover charge during their peak hours. Such bars often feature entertainment, which may be a live band or a popular disk jockey.

The term "bar" is derived from the specialized counter on which drinks are served. The "back bar" is a set of shelves of glasses and bottles behind that counter. In some establishments, the back bar is elaborately decorated with woodwork, etched glass, mirrors, and lights.

There have been many names throughout history for establishments where people gather to drink alcoholic beverages. Even when an establishment uses a different name, such as "tavern," the area of the establishment where the bartender serves alcoholic beverages is normally called "the bar."

There were prohibitions of alcoholic beverages in the first half of the 20th century in several countries, including Finland, Iceland, Norway, and the United States. In the United States, illegal bars during Prohibition were called speakeasies or blind pigs.

Laws in many jurisdictions prohibit minors from entering a bar. Cities and towns usually have legal restrictions on where bars may be located and on the types of alcohol they may serve to their customers.

Some Muslim countries, including Brunei, Iran, Libya, Saudi Arabia, and the UAE emirate of Sharjah, prohibit bars for religious reasons. Some other Muslim countries, including Bahrain, Qatar, and the United Arab Emirates, do allow bars but only permit non-Muslims to drink in them.

Christmas-time always puts people in a mood of nostalgia and love. You must evoke these feelings in your guests and work for those tips! Below are SEVEN of the powerful tips and tricks I implement in all of my Christmas Parties!

1. Get in the Mood—It's Christmas! Let's get excited about it! I want you to try this: Give your guest their drink, look them in the eye and say, "Merry Christmas." ...and mean it! Because we don't say it anymore! Everyone is worried about being "P.C." But take the time to say some kind, genuine words to your clients and spread that Christmas Cheer!

2. Charge More—Do you remember your High School Economics? As the Demand increases (more parties in December) so do your prices! Do NOT be afraid to charge more for your services this December. If you are a client looking for a bartender this December, it is going to be hard! Everyone is booked! So take advantage of that and hold out for the highest bidder! On a side note, you should be increasing your prices as you get closer and closer to the 25th and of course, charge AT LEAST TRIPLE on New Year's Eve!!

3. Dress Up—This Christmas, I am dressing up for a Tropical X-Mas Theme as well as a Tacky Sweater Party. For my other events, I will be wearing AT LEAST a Santa Hat! What will you be doing to make you stand out?!

4. Decorate Your Tip Jar—This Christmas, my tip jar will actually be decorated to look like a stocking! Instead of candy and gifts, this stocking will have tons of cash! Even better! How can you decorate your tip jar to make it look more festive? Try wrapping it in a small wreath or adding christmas lights.

5. Decorate Your Bar—You can also add some Christmas decorations to your bar. Some wreathing and lights will go along way and help everyone get in the mood!

6. Give Gifts/Treats—'Tis the Season! Take the time to put up a bowl of candy(like Candy Canes!), some Christmas cookies or even little gifts. What if you had a small little tree on the bar, with little mini presents. Each present was a wrapped up mini bottle of liquor that the guest could open and keep!

7. Customized Drinks/drink Menu—You MUST have some Holiday Cocktails for your guests.

Bars and Entertainment

A bar's owners and managers will choose the bar's name, décor, drink menu, lighting, and other elements which they think will attract a certain kind of patron. However, they have only limited influence over who patronizes their establishment. Thus, a bar intended for one demographic can become popular with another. For example, a gay bar with a dance floor might, over time, attract an increasingly straight clientele. Or a blues bar may become a biker bar if most its patrons are bikers.

A cocktail lounge is an up scale bar that is typically located within a hotel, restaurant, or airport. A wine bar is an elegant bar that serves only wine (no beer or liquor). Patrons of these bars may taste wines before deciding to buy them. Some wine bars also serve snacks. A dive bar is a very informal bar.

Bars categorized by the kind of entertainment they offer include:

- Topless bars, where topless female employees dance or serve drinks
- Sports bars, where sports fans watch games on large-screen televisions
- Salsa bars, where patrons dance to Latin salsa music
- Dance bars, which have a dance floor where patrons dance to recorded music. But if a dance

bar has a large dance floor and hires well-known professional DJs, it is considered to be nightclub or discothèque.

Patrons

Bars categorized by the kind of patrons who frequent them include:

- Biker bars, which are bars frequented by motorcycle enthusiasts and (in some regions) motorcycle club members
- Gay bars, where gay men or women dance and socialize
- Cop bars, where off-duty law enforcement agents gather
- Singles bars where (mostly) unmarried people of both sexes can meet and socialize

Managing Your Own Bar

So you want to open a bar. Sounds like a fun way to make a living. Well, it is and it isn't. The following is most definitely not a comprehensive check list for opening a bar. Your business plan will provide that. This is more of a reality check before you get started.

First, you do have some experience in the food and beverage business, right? And not from the bar stool side. Meaning you've been a bartender or a server. I'm not including management in this because management may know how to do the paper work and run the numbers, that doesn't necessarily mean knowing how to properly serve customers or make an adequate margarita. People who can serve the public day after day have great people skills. And that's what running a bar is about. People. Do you like people, even when they've had one too many? Drunks are very hard to take on a day to day basis. And you'll see many of the same faces every day, hear the same stories, day after day, week after week. Can you do it?

You say you won't be the one behind the bar or serving food, you'll be hiring others to do that for you. Don't believe it. Yes, you'll need staff, but bar patrons, especially in a local bar, want to see the owner, not just the hired help. It's an every day job, smiling, chatting at tables, milling around to see that everyone's happy, breaking up heated discussions and lover's spats, being a shoulder to cry on or the source of encouraging words.

There will also be those days... and many of them in a bar... when the help doesn't show up. Who takes over when the bartender, server, or cook calls off? Unless you have the resources of a faithful staff who are willing to come in on a day off, you take over. You're the owner, the one in charge. The one who sees that everything runs smoothly and that patrons are served promptly and well. Jack of a trades, you'll know how to mix drinks, set a table and carry a tray, and how to cook every item on the menu.

Do you have a family? Owning a bar when there are small children at home isn't easy. You need to be at work most of the hours your establishment is open... at least 12 to 16 hours a day. You may open the bar at 10AM and not get home until dawn's early light. That doesn't leave much time for family life. It can be done easiest if you live close to your business, allowing you to run home for meals or tucking the kids in at night. Of course, meal time at home is also meal time at your bar and the kid's bedtime could be one of the busiest hours at your business.

Those are some personal things to think about. Others are the nuts and bolts of the business, the actual business side of running a bar.

If you're opening a new venture, is a license available? The Alcohol Beverage Commission of your state will have the answer to that question. In Indiana, population determines the number of licenses permitted. Population increases will allow for more licenses. If you're buying an established business, is the license current and up to date? Drinking establishments have been closed and patrons ushered out the door until lapsed licenses are renewed.

Again, if it's a new establishment, do you have a location picked out? Check zoning to see if you can open a bar there. In Indiana, a business that serves alcoholic beverages must be a certain distance from schools and churches. Check you local and state zoning laws.

Who will be your suppliers for beer, liquor, soft drinks, food supplies, paper supplies, cleaning services, insurance? There may not be any options about who supplies your alcoholic beverages. In Indiana, for instance, suppliers are limited to certain areas of distribution. But you'll want to check prices, quality, and dependability of other products and services.

Before you can order supplies, you need to know how much of what to order. A grand opening or re-opening will probably call for a heavy supply of booze and food. What sort of food will you serve? Sandwiches and fries, full meals, lunch specials? My thought on this is to avoid having an extensive menu. Serve only limited items, but be absolutely certain that they're the best in town. Make your burger bigger and juicer, serve only a generous cut of prime rib, use real butter and good dinner rolls, offer all the toppings for baked potatoes, use crisp, fresh chips for nachos, don't offer endless types of hot wings... just the favorite of the area, use onion or other specialty buns for sandwiches. See how that goes... your food has something special that makes it the best in town.

Who's going to work in your establishment? Do check references when hiring staff. Does the bartender have the awareness to know when a patron has been over-served? Can she tell the patron he's cut off without starting a riot...

as in, diplomatically? In actual fact, this rarely works. No one wants to be told that their evening is over, that's it's coffee or nothing. Be prepared to back up your bartender when this happens, as it surely will. Mixing drinks and pouring beer are skills that can be learned and improved with practice. More important to your business is the personality of the bartender. A surly one will run off business as sure as the sun will rise tomorrow. Hire the person who smiles.

Those same traits are what you'll look for in hiring servers. And the ability to take food orders accurately, serve promptly, and get the food and drinks to the right people at the right table. That's not as easy as it would seem when the place is packed and everyone came in at the same time. A good server is worth his or her weight in gold many times over.

Who's cooking? Hire a cook, not a chef. Unless, of course, you'll be serving upscale meals. If you're looking for someone to get the food out quickly and properly, hire an experienced line cook. The cook should be responsible for ordering kitchen supplies, supervising helpers, food quality, and cleanliness in the handling and preparation of food.

Liability. People drink and drive. If a person causes an accident after drinking in your establishment, you could be held liable. You need insurance, but how much? The best advice is to consult an attorney. And be certain all of your staff knows how to tell when a patron has had too much.

Music and dancing is part of the fun in a bar. Live music, a dj, or just the juke box? More decisions to make. Is there room for a dance floor? Are there state or local regulations prohibiting dancing? Is there a law or regulation regarding noise? And then there is ASCAP, The American Society of Composers, Authors and Publishers. ASCAP protects the rights of member songwriters, composers, lyricists, etc., by requiring a license to play or perform members music in public. Check this out with your attorney. Music and dancing bring business to your establishment, so you'll have to pay for the licensing, if it's required.

Still want to own a bar? There are as many headaches as there are rewards. But you'll be providing jobs, income, services, and entertainment to your community while enjoying the way you make a living. So maybe the rewards outnumber the headaches.

Bar (counter)

The counter at which drinks are served by a bartender is called "the bar". This term is applied, as a synecdoche, to drinking establishments called "bars". The bar typically stores a variety of beers, wines, liquors, and non-alcoholic ingredients, and is organized to facilitate the bartender's work.

The word "bar" in this context was already in use by 1592 at the latest, as the dramatist Robert Greene referred to one in his *A Noteable Discovery of Coosnage*. However, it has been suggested that the method of serving from a counter was invented by Isambard Kingdom Brunel, the great Victorian engineer, as a means of more quickly serving the sudden rush of customers caused by passenger trains arriving at the refreshment rooms at Swindon railway station while the Great Western Railway trains changed locomotives. It has also been claimed that the first bar to serve alcohol was installed at the Great Western Hotel on Paddington station, London. Counters for serving other types of food and drink may also be called bars. Examples include salad bars, sushi bars, and sundae bars.

MAXIMISE YOUR PROFIT

Today, dollar-stretching is once again a valuable skill, especially when scrutinizing monthly and annual expenses.

You want to channel the thrift of your forebears to wring every possible drop of value from the dollars you spend.To that end, here are a few ways to maximize the value you get from your bar association dues.

If you are like most lawyers, you belong to one or two bar associations. You pay your bar dues each year, attend a few CLE programs and don't think about your membership much beyond that. The thing is, there's a lot more value in your association membership just waiting for you to scoop it up. And since you pay the full amount of dues anyway, why not get the full amount of value?

Six Tips to Get You Started

1. Find out if the bar has a practice management advisor **on staff.** If so, use him or her to help you with whatever technology, marketing, ethics or management issue is presently causing you to lose sleep at night.

2. Take part in your association's pro bono activities. You will get the opportunity to help people, improve the image of the profession, network with your peers and shake up your daily routine. Plus it's good karma.

3. Utilize the discussion boards or e-mail listserves. It gives you the chance to crowd-source a thorny legal issue, discuss developments in your practice area and just gather around the watercooler to chat, even if you work alone.

4. Take advantage of your bar's free or discounted CLE programs for members. Make them a networking opportunity in addition to a learning opportunity by introducing yourself to a stranger at lunch and mingling at the breaks instead of fielding calls from the office.

5. Check out free legal research tools. Some bars provide free legal research tools like Casemaker or Fastcase. See if you still need that expensive subscription or if you can use your free bar-based tool to reduce your costs.

6. Volunteer for a leadership position. From the board of governors to committee chairs, a key thing that differentiates bar associations from consulting companies and private businesses catering to lawyers is that your association belongs to *you*—and is waiting for you to take a turn at the helm to lead it.

Australia

In Australia the major form of licenced commercial alcohol outlet from the colonial period to the present was the pub, a local variant of the English original. Until the 1970s, Australian pubs were traditionally organised into gender-segregated drinking areas—the "public bar" was only open to men, while the 'lounge bar' or 'saloon bar' served both men and women (i.e. mixed drinking).

This distinction was gradually eliminated as anti-discrimination legislation and women's rights activism broke down the concept of a public drinking area accessible to only men. Where two bars still exist in the one establishment, one (that derived from the 'public bar') will be more downmarket while the other (deriving from the 'lounge bar') will be more upmarket. Over time, with the introduction of gaming machines into hotels, many 'lounge bars' have or are being converted into gaming rooms.

Beginning in the mid-1950s, the formerly strict state liquor licencing laws were progressively relaxed and reformed, with the result that pub trading hours were extended. This was in part to eliminate the social problems associated with early closing times—notably the infamous "Six O'Clock Swill" — and the thriving trade in "sly grog" (illicit alcohol sales). More licenced liquor outlets began to appear, including retail "bottle shops" (over-the-counter bottle sales were previously only available at pubs and were strictly controlled).

Particularly in Sydney, a new class of licenced premises, the wine bar, appeared; there alcohol could be served on the proviso that it was provided in tandem with a meal. These venues became very popular in the late 1960s and early 1970s and many offered free entertainment, becoming an important facet of the Sydney music scene in that period.

In the major Australian cities today there is a large and diverse bar scene with a range of ambiences, modes and styles catering for every echelon of cosmopolitan society.

Canada

Canada has absorbed many of the public house traditions common in the UK, such as the drinking of dark ales and stouts. Canada adopted the UK-style tavern (also adopted by the U.S), which was the most popular type of bar throughout the 1960s and 1970s, especially for working class people. Canadian taverns, which can still be found in remote regions of Northern Canada, have long tables with benches lining the sides. Patrons in these taverns often order beer in large quart bottles and drink inexpensive "bar brand" Canadian rye whisky. In some provinces, taverns used to have separate entrances for men and women.

Canada has adopted many of the newer U.S. bar traditions (such as the "biker bar", and the "sports bar") of the last decades. As a result the term "bar" has often come to be differentiated with the term "pub", in that bars are usually 'themed' and often have a dance floor (such as a dance bar), as opposed to establishments which call themselves pubs, which are often much more similar to a British tavern in style. Before the mid-1980s most "bar" like establishments that sold alcohol were simply referred to as taverns, regardless of what they looked like or what they sold.

As with any major lifestyle trend that occurs in the U.S. the "bar" trend promptly spread to Canada. Canadian sports bars are usually decorated with merchandise and paraphernalia featuring the local hockey team, and patrons watch the games on large-screen televisions. Starting in the mid-1990s taverns started to take on the look, feel and even the names of the U.K type pubs. A simple example would be the name "The Fox and Fiddle" as a pub name, whereas names like these rarely existed before. There is huge proportion of bars compared to pubs.

Legal restrictions on bars are set by the Canadian provinces and territories, which has led to a great deal of variety. While some provinces have been very restrictive with their bar regulation, setting strict closing times and banning the removal of alcohol from the premises, other provinces have been more liberal. Closing times generally run from 2:00 to 4:00 a.m.

In Nova Scotia, particularly in Halifax, there was, until the 1980s, a very distinct system of gender-based laws were in effect for decades. Taverns, bars, halls, and other classifications differentiated whether it was exclusively for men or women, men with invited women, vice-versa, or mixed. After this fell by the wayside, the issue of water closets led many powder rooms in taverns being either constructed later, or in kitchens or upstairs halls where plumbing allowed, and the same in former sitting rooms for men's facilities.

India

Bars in India are mainly clustered in metro cities, like Delhi, Mumbai, Bangalore, Hyderabad, Goa Manipal etc. Bangalore is sometimes referred to as the city of pubs as there are over 200 bars and pubs located in the city. The state of Goa also has a large number of bars and pubs because of tourism. The rest of the country has very few bar formats. Mostly, drinks are served in establishments such as restaurants. Locally made liquor (fenny, toddy etc.) is also exclusively sold at establishments. They don't serve traditional liquor but usually serve several snacks and food. These establishments are usually run-down, and their clientele consists mainly of working-class people.

More recently, bars are showing up in smaller cities; but, these establishments cater to a mostly male clientele and are unlike the social hubs of the west. For example, in Chandigarh, one of the most modern city of India, administration has developed Taverns where people can buy liquor at market price and have it along with snacks being served in a decent sitting restaurant that accompanies the wine shop.

In Manipal , many bars serve patrons standing at the counter — no seating arrangements are provided. All the bars are crowded with students

In the last few years, many international brands have entered the market, like 'Hard Rock Cafe', 'TGI Friday's', Ruby Tuesday's', Pop Tate's, 'Ministry of Sound(MOS)', etc. Similar chains of bars are now starting to emerge from within the country. Shalom, Laidbackwaters, Geoffrey's Dhadkkan at Solan, Himachal Pradesh and All Sports Bar are among the few popular ones.

Italy

In Italy, a "bar" is a place more similar to a café, where people go during the morning or the afternoon, usually to take a coffee, a cappuccino, a hot chocolate and eat some kind of snack like pastries and sandwiches (*panini* or *tramezzini*). However, any kind of alcoholic beverages are served. Opening hours vary: some establishments are open very early in the morning and close relatively early in the evening; others, especially if next to a theater or a cinema, may be open until late at night. In larger cities like Milan, Rome, Turin or Genoa, many larger bars are also restaurants and disco clubs. Many Italian bars have introduced a so-called "aperitivo" time in the evening, in which everyone who purchases an alcoholic drink then has free access to a usually abundant buffet of cold dishes like pasta salads, vegetables and various types of appetizers.

Spain

Bars in Spain are very common and form an important part in Spanish culture. In Spain it is common for a town to have many bars and even to have several lined up in the same street. Most bars have a section of the street or plaza outside with tables and chairs with parasols if the weather allows it. Spanish bars are also known for serving a wide range of sandwiches (bocadillos), as well as snacks called tapas or pinchos.

Tapas and pinchos may be offered to customers in two ways, either complementary to order a drink or in some cases there are charged independently, either case this is usually clearly indicated to bar customers by display of wall information, on menus and price lists. The anti-smoking law has entered in effect January 1st 2011 and since that date it is prohibited to smoke in bars and restaurants as well as all other indoor areas, closed commercial and state owned facilities are now smoke free areas.

Spain is the country with the highest ratio of bars/ population with almost 6 bars per thousand inhabitants, that's 3 times UK's ratio and 4 times Germany's, and it alone has double the number of bars than the oldest of the 15-members of the European Union. The meaning of the word 'bar' in Spain, however, does not have the negative connotation inherent in the same word in many other languages. For Spanish people a bar is essentially a meeting place, and not necessarily a place to engage in the consumption of alcoholic beverages. As a result, children are normally allowed into bars, and it's common to see families in bars during week-ends of the end of the day. In small towns, the 'bar' may constitute the very center of social life, and it's customary that, after social events, such as the Sunday catholic mass, people go to bars, including seniors and children alike.

United Kingdom

In the UK bars are either areas that serve alcoholic drinks within establishments such as hotels, restaurants, universities, or are a particular type of establishment which serves alcoholic drinks such as wine bars, "style bars", private membership only bars. However the main type of establishment selling alcohol for consumption on the premises is the public house or *pub*. Some bars are similar to nightclubs in that they feature loud music, subdued lighting, or operate a dress code and admissions policy, with inner city bars generally having door staff at the entrance.

'Bar' also designates a separate drinking area within a pub. Until recent years most pubs had two or more bars - very often the Public bar, and the Saloon Bar, where the decor was better and prices were sometimes higher. The designations of the bars varied regionally. In the last two decades many pub interiors have been opened up into single spaces, which some people regret as it loses the flexibility, intimacy and traditional feel of a multi-roomed public house. One of the last dive bars in London was underneath the Kings Head pub in Gerrard Street, Soho.

United States

In the United States, legal distinctions often exist between restaurants and bars, and even between types of bars. These distinctions vary from state to state, and even among municipalities. *Beer bars* (sometimes called taverns or pubs) are legally restricted to selling only beer, and possibly wine or cider. *Liquor bars* also sell hard liquor.

Bars are sometimes exempt from smoking bans that restaurants are subject to, even if those restaurants have liquor licenses. The distinction between a restaurant that serves liquor and a bar is usually made by the percentage of revenue earned from selling liquor, although increasingly, smoking bans include bars too.

In most places, bars are prohibited from selling alcoholic beverages *to go* and this makes them clearly different from liquor stores. Some brewpubs and wineries can serve alcohol *to go,* but under the rules applied to a liquor store. In some areas, such as New Orleans and parts of Las Vegas and Savannah, Georgia, open containers of alcohol may be prepared *to go.* This kind of restriction is usually dependent on an open container law. In Pennsylvania and Ohio, bars may sell six packs of beer "to-go" in original (sealed) containers by obtaining a take-out license.

New Jersey permits all forms of packaged goods to be sold at bars, and permits packaged beer and wine to be sold at any time on-premises sales of alcoholic beverages are allowed. Historically, the western United States featured saloons. Many saloons survive in the western United States, though their services and features have changed with the times. Newer establishments have been built in the saloon style to duplicate the feeling of the older establishments.Many Irish or British-themed "pubs" exist throughout United States and Canada and in some continental European countries.

Nightclub

A nightclub (also known simply as a club, discothèque or disco) is an entertainment venue which usually operates late into the night. A nightclub is generally distinguished from bars, pubs or taverns by the inclusion of a dance floor and a DJ booth, where a DJ plays recorded dance, hip hop, rock, reggae and pop music.

The music in nightclubs is either live bands or, more commonly, a mix of songs played by a DJ through a powerful PA system. Most clubs or club nights cater to certain music genres, such as techno, house music, trance, heavy metal, garage, hip hop, salsa, dancehall, Drum and Bass, Dubstep or soca music. Many clubs also promote playing the Top 40 which has most of the night playing the most broadcast songs of the previous week.

Many nightclubs choose who can enter, on bases other than just age, e.g. dress code and guest list. This is used to make their status as a nightclub more "exclusive". Quite often, there are no clear policies governing entry to a nightclub, thereby allowing the doormen to deny entry to anybody at their discretion.

Cover Charge

In most cases, entering a night club requires a flat fee called a cover charge. Early arrivers and women may have their cover charge waived or reduced (in the United Kingdom, this latter option is illegal under the Sex Discrimination Act 1975 but the law is rarely enforced and open violations are frequent). Friends of the doorman or the club owner may gain free entrance.

Sometimes, especially at larger clubs in continental European countries, one only gets a pay card at the entrance, on which all money spent in the discothèque (often including the entrance fee) is marked. Sometimes, entrance fee and cloakroom costs are paid by cash and only the drinks in the club are paid using a pay card.

Guestlist

Many nightclubs operate a "guestlist" that allows certain attendees to enter the club for free, or at a reduced rate. Some nightclubs have a range of unpublicised guestlist options ranging from free, to reduced, to full price with line by-pass privileges only. Nightclub goers that are on the guestlist usually have a separate queue and possibly a separate entrance to the one used by full price paying attendees. It is not uncommon for the guestlist line-up to be as long or longer than the full-paying or ticketed queues. Some nightclubs allow clubbers to register for the guestlist through their websites.

Dress Code

Many nightclubs enforce a dress code in order to ensure a certain type of clientele is in attendance at the venue. Some upscale nightclubs ban attendees from wearing trainers or jeans, while other nightclubs will advertise a vague "dress to impress" dress code that allows the bouncers to discriminate at will against those vying for entry to the club.

Many exceptions are made to nightclub dress codes, with denied entry usually reserved for the most glaring rule breakers or those thought to be unsuitable for the party. Certain niche clubs like fetish nightclubs may apply a leather-only, rubber-only or fantasy dress code. The dress code criterion is often an excuse for discriminatory practices, such as in the case of Carpenter v. Limelight Entertainment Ltd.

Association

Many nightclubs will only allow entry by association. A number of gay nightclubs that prefer to cater to an exclusively male clientele will deny entry to a group of lesbians but will welcome a lesbian with a number of gay friends.

Early Growth

From about 1900 to 1920, working class Americans would gather at honky tonks or juke joints to dance to music played on a piano or a jukebox. During US Prohibition, nightclubs went underground as illegal speakeasy bars. With the repeal of Prohibition in February 1933, nightclubs were revived, such as New York's Stork Club, 21 Club, El Morocco and the Copacabana. These nightclubs featured big bands (there were no DJ's).

In Occupied France, jazz and bebop music, and the jitterbug dance were banned by the Nazis as decadent American *influences*, so members of the French underground met at hidden underground basement dance clubs called *discotheques* where they danced to American swing music, which a DJ played on a single turntable when a jukebox was not available. These "discotheques" were also patronized by anti-Vichy youth called zazous. There were also underground discotheques in Nazi Germany patronized by anti-Nazi youth called the swing kids.

In Harlem, the Cotton Club and Connie's Inn were popular venues for white audiences. Before 1953 and even some years thereafter, most bars and nightclubs used a jukebox or mostly live bands. In Paris, at a club named "Whisky à Gogo", founded in 1947,Régine in 1953 laid down a dance-floor, suspended coloured lights and replaced the juke-box with two turntables which she operated herself so there would be no breaks between the music. The Whisky à Gogo set into place the standard elements of the modern post World War II discothèque-style nightclub. In the early 1960s, Mark Birley opened a members-only discothèque nightclub, Annabel's, in Berkeley Square, London. In 1962, the Peppermint Lounge in New York City became popular and is the place where go-go dancing originated. However, the first rock and roll generation preferred rough and tumble bars and taverns to nightclubs, and the nightclub did not attain mainstream popularity until the 1970s disco era.

1970s: Disco

By the late 1970s many major US cities had thriving disco club scenes which were centered around discothèques, nightclubs, and private loft parties where DJs would play disco hits through powerful PA systems for the dancers. The DJs played "... a smooth mix of long single records to keep people 'dancing all night long'" Some of the most prestigious clubs had elaborate lighting systems that throbbed to the beat of the music.

Some cities had disco dance instructors or dance schools which taught people how to do popular disco dances such as "touch dancing", the "hustle" and the "cha-cha-cha".

There were also disco fashions that discothèque-goers wore for nights out at their local disco, such as sheer, flowing Halston dresses for women and shiny polyester Qiana shirts for men. Disco clubs and "...hedonistic loft parties" had a club culture which had many Italian-American, African American, gay and Hispanic people.

In addition to the dance and fashion aspects of the disco club scene, there was also a thriving drug subculture, particularly for recreational drugs that would enhance the experience of dancing to the loud music and the flashing lights, such as cocaine (nicknamed "blow"), amyl nitrite "poppers", and the "...other quintessential 1970s club drug Quaalude, which suspended motor coordination and turned one's arms and legs to Jell-O". The "massive quantities of drugs ingested in discothèques by newly liberated gay men produced the next cultural phenomenon of the disco era: rampant promiscuity and public sex. While the dance floor was the central arena of seduction, actual sex usually took place in the nether regions of the disco: bathroom stalls, exit stairwells, and so on. In other cases the disco became a kind of "main course" in a hedonist's menu for a night out."

Famous 1970s discothèques included "...cocaine-filled celeb hangouts such as Manhattan's "Studio 54", which was operated by Steve Rubell and Ian Schrager. Studio 54 was notorious for the hedonism that went on within; the balconies were known for sexual encounters, and drug use was rampant. Its dance floor was decorated with an image of the "Man in the Moon" that included an animated cocaine spoon. Other famous 1970s discothèques in New York City included "Xenon", "The Loft", the "Paradise Garage", and "Aux Puces", one of the first gay disco bars. In San Francisco, there was the Trocadero Transfer, the I-Beam, and the End Up.

By the early 1980s, the term "disco" had largely fallen out of favor in North America.

1980s New York, London and Europe

During the 1980s, during the New Romantic movement, London had a vibrant nightclub scene, which included clubs like The Blitz, the Batcave, the Camden Palace and Club for Heroes. Both music and fashion embraced the aesthetics of the movement. Bands included Depeche Mode, The Human League, Duran Duran, Blondie, Eurythmics and Ultravox. Reggae-influenced bands included Boy George and Culture Club, and electronic vibe bands included Visage. At London nightclubs, young men would often wear make-up and young women would wear men's suits.

The largest UK cities like Newcastle, Liverpool, Quadrant Park and 051, Swansea, Manchester (The Haçienda) and several key European places like Paris (Les Bains Douches), Berlin, Ibiza (Pacha), Rimini etc. also played a significant role in the evolution of clubbing, DJ culture and nightlife.

Significant New York nightclubs of the period were Area, Danceteria, and The Limelight.

Growth During 1990s and 2000s

In Europe and North America, nightclubs play disco-influenced dance music such as house music, techno, and other dance music styles such as electronica and trance. Most nightclubs in the U.S. major cities play hip hop, house and trance music. These clubs are generally the largest and most frequented of all of the different types of clubs. The emergence of the "superclub" created a global phenomenon, with Ministry of Sound (London), Cream (Liverpool) and Pacha (Ibiza).

In most other languages, nightclubs are referred to as "discos" or "discothèques" (French: *discothèque;* Italian and Spanish: *discoteca, antro* (common in Mexico only), and "boliche" (common in Argentina only), "discos" is commonly used in all others in Latinamerica; German: *Disko* or *Diskothek*). In Japanese Ç0£0[1]0[3]0, *disuko* refers to an older, smaller, less fashionable venue; while ¯0é0Ö0, *kurabu* refers to a more recent, larger, more popular venue. The term *night* is used to refer to an evening focusing on a specific genre, such as "retro music night" or a "singles night."

A recent trend in the North American and European nightclub industry is the usage of video. Instead of audio-only, DJ's are now using video and "mixing" music videos and related songs together in an audio/visual presentation.

TIPS FOR YOUR NIGHTCLUB FLYERS

There are so many things you can do with printing today that will enhance the look and feel of your flyers. Since these are going to be your advertising and marketing tools, it is going to be very important to design them and lay them out the right way. Here we will take a look at a few different ways to make your nightclub flyers stand out from the rest and be an investment you will profit from.

First off, be sure that you are using a professional printer. They will print your nightclub flyers better than you could and the finished product will look much more polished. You want your potential customers to have a good feeling about your club from the start.

Use a heavy card stock so that the flyer feels different in someone's hand. You can change the texture of your paper or make your flyers slightly smaller than usual to draw more attention to them. Whatever you can think of to make someone pick up your flyer and read it is good.

You can also use nightclub flyers to announce special events your club is having. Another popular thing to do is add a coupon or free gift with the purchase of something, etc. You are ultimately going to need a flyer that offers the public something. People want to feel as though they know about your club before they actually enter it. Your club card flyers should reflect the style and nature of your nightclub; readers should feel a certain way about it once they have read your flyer.

As far as distributing your flyers goes, you can do this in several different ways. First, you can always use them as a direct mail piece. You may want to send them to a targeted area somewhere in close proximity to your club so that the recipients will be more likely to visit. You can also use your nightclub flyers as pieces to stick onto someone's windshield or leave in between their doors. This will save you money on postage, but keep in mind that some people see this type of distribution as 'junk mail' and don't take time to really read through it. This is why your design and the feel of your flyers are so important.

So, when promoting your nightclub it is a great idea to use professionally printed nightclub flyers. You must make sure that your flyers stand out from all others. If you are able to get noticed and have someone actually read your flyer, you have succeeded.

4

THE GROWTH STRATEGIES OF EQUIPMENT AND SUPPLIES

The Hotel and Restaurant Equipment industry manufactures specialized equipment for use in commercial and institutional kitchens and residential accommodations, including hotels, restaurants, resorts, catering businesses, schools and colleges, hospitals, nursing homes and assisted living facilities, and similar settings.

Major product categories include: ovens, stoves, ranges and other devices for heating food or keeping it warm; refrigerators, freezers and other devices for keeping food cold, including refrigerated and freezer-type display cases, and refrigerated equipment for dispensing beer and carbonated beverages; ice-making machines, dishwashers; vacuum cleaners; washing and drying machines for clothes, table and bed linens, etc., porcelain and other ware for serving food; and specialized furniture for hotel, restaurant, and other commercial applications.

Also covered in this category, but difficult to document statistically are small commercial kitchen appliances, hair dryers, clothes irons, cutlery, and similar products.

Industry Overview and Competitiveness

More than 500 companies of all sizes manufacture hotel and restaurant equipment in the United States. Many of the leading brands of high-value product types are concentrated in the hands of large corporate manufacturers with multiple brands and subsidiaries, such as Illinois Tool Works, Manitowoc Company, Inc., and True Food Service Equipment.

Frequently, these and other large manufacturers produce equipment for preparing hot foods and beverages, or for storing and displaying cold foods and beverages, as well as dishwashers, vacuum cleaners, and other motor-driven devices. There are also numerous small and medium-sized manufacturers, frequently offering innovative products or serving particular market niches.

Major end-users of hotel and restaurant equipment include restaurant and hotel chains, schools and colleges, hospitals and other residential health-care providers, commercial caterers, and other institutional customers. Franchise restaurant chains, especially in the fast-food sector, are especially important for large-scale sales and repeat business.

Because the hotel and restaurant markets depend heavily on discretionary spending, the market for equipment is especially sensitive to economic downturns. State and local government end-users, such as schools and colleges, are also sensitive to economic conditions that reduce tax revenues on which their budgets depend, although other institutional end-users may not be quite so vulnerable.

Global Competitiveness

The hotel and restaurant equipment industry is a mature and highly competitive global business. Major markets for hotel restaurant equipment include North America, the European Union, East Asia, and the Middle East. U.S. exports grew steadily between 2004 and 2008, totaling $1.8 billion last year. International competition is strong in this industry sector, however, and imports in 2009 were worth $2.1 billion.

Leading U.S. manufacturers compete with counterparts from Italy, Germany, Sweden, Japan, and other developed industrialized nations. Conditions in more populous and affluent markets often lead manufacturers to localize manufacturing. Both the volume of local sales and specific national standards and other requirements for electric current, natural gas connections, food safety and so on are some of the reasons for localizing production.

Domestic Competitiveness

With its large and affluent population, the United States has tens of thousands of hotels, restaurants, and other commercial and institutional end-users of hotel and restaurant equipment. Hundreds of domestic and international firms serve this market, both from domestic manufacturing operations and with imports. Major U.S. manufacturers include Illinois Tool Works, Inc., Manitowoc Company, Inc., True Food Service Equipment, Cambroon Manufacturing Company, and the NACCO Housewares Group, to name a few. Leading foreign manufacturers doing business in the United States include ALI SpA (Italy), AB Electrolux (Sweden), Franke Holding AG (Switzerland), Hoshizaki Electric Company, Ltd. (Japan), Meiko Maschinenebau GmbH (Germany).

Domestic Environment

The hotel and restaurant industries have been negatively affected by the economic downturn that began in late 2007. The recession has cut Americans' discretionary spending on restaurant meals and hotel stays significantly. Business travel has also declined, adding to the drop in business for commercial end-users of hotel and restaurant equipment.

Food safety remains a key issue for all commercial and institutional restaurant and catering businesses. Ensuring that their products are designed to meet high standards of safety and sanitation is essential for companies in the hotel and restaurant equipment industry.

Sustainability is also a growing concern for U.S. manufacturers. Hotel and restaurant operations necessarily involve extensive consumption of energy and water and produce significant volumes of solid and liquid waste. Individual manufacturers increasingly design their products to make more efficient use of energy and water and reduce their customers' output of waste.

The leading U.S. trade association for manufacturers of hotel and restaurant equipment is the North American Association of Food Equipment Manufacturers (NAFEM). With more than 600 members, NAFEM represents foodservice equipment and supply manufacturers "that provide products for food preparation, cooking, storage and table service."

The biennial NAFEM Show, held in odd-numbered years in cities throughout the United States, attracts as many 20,000 foodservice professionals and more than 600 exhibitors. NAFEM has participated in the International Buyer Program in the past, most recently in 2004.

The National Restaurant Association also offers membership to manufacturers of equipment and supplies for the restaurant and food service industry. The National Restaurant Association is a long-time participant in the International Buyer Program.

This industry's relationship with the Department of Commerce goes back decades. In the early days of Federal Government trade promotion, DIBA (ITA's predecessor) worked closely with the Barbecue King Co. and literally put the company into the export market. For many years, the company was the "poster child" success story demonstrating how exporting using Commerce services could be profitable for the small and medium size U.S. company (unfortunately, Barbecue King today is a British company).

Later, DOC worked closely with the industry to help the Germans prepare for the ill-fated Munich Olympics. Still later, DOC worked with the industry to help a wide variety of U.S. companies penetrate the Japanese market. In recent years, the relationship has been limited to the industry's participation in the International Buyer Program.

World's Ten Top Hotel Rooms?

Have you stayed in a sexy hotel room? Tell us about it using the comment form below

1. PLAYHOUSE ROOM SohoHouse, New York—It's impossible to walk into these bedrooms, with their flagrant display of extravagance and generosity, and not be filled with a sense of fun. They're like a little devil on your shoulder, persuasively listing arguments why you need to loosen your corsets and behave very badly indeed.

There are the gorgeous 7ft hand-carved beds, with curves as coquettish as the flirtiest of French flirts, piled high with the plumpest pillows and dreamiest, flounce-inducing linens, with antique chandeliers overhead and vast dinosaur-egg stone baths perched provocatively at their bases.

And if, by some sad circumstance, you're still at a loss for inspiration, raid the minibar, which stocks everything from Ben & Jerry ice cream to love dice for some grown-up roll play. From £505, room-only; 00 1 212 627 9800, www.sohohouseny.com

2. BANDA 5 Beho Beho, Tanzania—You can't help feeling for the honeymooners who come to Beho Beho. How, in the rest of their married lives, will they ever equal the lubricious thrill of staying here? You're in a grand banda, a huge thatched cottage with polished flagstone floors, exquisite antique furniture, an open-air stone shower and a vast, crisp-linened, muslin-draped bed.

Best of all, the front is completely open, giving an enormous view over a valley where giraffes, impalas, lions and leopards roam. It's an irresistibly sexy cocktail of drama, luxury and an edge of danger - in theory, there's nothing to stop those leopards dropping in for a midnight snack.

In practice, they stay well clear, though the elephants sometimes parade past on.their way for a drink from the swimming pool. There are just eight bandas: go for number five for that out-in-the-wilds feel. A four-night break starts at £2,319pp, full-board, with flights; 020 8232 9777, www.expertafrica.com

3. DOUBLE MURANO Murano, Paris—While Paris remains a city for lovers, most of its hotels cling to a concept of "romantic" and "sexy" that translates as "Louis XV's favourite brothel". Not so the Murano, in the Marais, a far more contemporary interpretation of what might tickle a couple's erogenous zones. Unlike some other lounge-lizardy hotels (hello, Costes), the bon-chic vibe doesn't evaporate as soon as you leave the public areas, the Murano's rooms being as fun and far-out as the retro-futurist lobby and bar.

As a self-proclaimed "Urban Resort", it has two suites with (small) outdoor heated pools, but they'll knock you back almost two grand a night. Opt instead for one of the Double Murano rooms (from about £330, room-only), with their raised podium beds and slate bathrooms, and you'll be more than satisfied. Murano Urban Resort; 00 33 1 42 70 20 00, www.muranoresort.com

4. THE GUARDROOM The Witchery, Edinburgh—There's an engraving of Queen Victoria overlooking the four-poster bed in the Guardroom suite. She looks, as usual, thoroughly disapproving - but this time she's got good reason, given the behaviour she's no doubt had to witness here. There's nowhere better set up for high-class high jinks.

Tucked away on the top floor of a 17th-century building off Castlehill, each of the five richly decorated rooms is more decadent than the last.

The antique double bath, with its enormous mirror, is especially thought-provoking. The dark and sensuous bedroom, meanwhile, is a riot of gilt, brocade and velvet - the style is sort of tartan harem. With champagne on arrival, it's sheer aristocratic decadence. It's not often that we bow to Dannii Minogue, but her description - "the perfect lust-den" - is unimprovable. Guardroom suite £295, B&B; 0131 225 5613, www.thewitchery.com

5. MACKA TREE The Caves, Negril—There's not a lot that's not sexy in Jamaica, and the Caves, on a Tracy Island-style honeycomb cliff just outside Negril, is one big bundle of "look you knowingly in the eye" sassiness. Its collection of 11 thatched love shacks operates to a permanent Bob Marley soundtrack, with Macka Tree the No 1 hit. We're talking an earthy, "doesn't have to try too hard" vibe here, so the room isn't huge or gadget-driven (there isn't even air-con - cool breezes have the edge when it comes to sensuality), but it's got that indefinable X factor - cool Caribbean colours, pretty fretwork and all-yours ocean views.

It also gives the male of the species maximum opportunity for machismo. He can flex and leap from one of the resort's cliff-edge diving platforms (the highest being 30ft) or find his inner caveman with dinner à deux in a flower-strewn volcanic grotto. From £275, all-inclusive; 00 1 876 957 0270, www.thecavesresort.com

6. ROOM 19 Riad el Fenn, Marrakesh—Moroccan riads (townhouses) were built for amorous assignations, with lots of dark nooks and crannies, as well as intimate courtyards to tempt you down the path of naughtiness. Riad el Fenn adds some quirky British styling to the mix. Room 19's sultry rendered dusky-pink walls twinkle with 3,000 teeny pieces of glass mosaic (as well as a splendid set of ink studies by Antony Gormley), while the Moroccan slippers that are yours to keep, the carved wooden doors and the handmade camel-bone ice buckets all feel breathtakingly exotic.

The bathroom sets out its intentions pretty clearly: an enormous glass shower with his-and-her shower heads, as well as an elegant pure-white cast-iron bath for drapier moments. Even walking across the floor is a sensual experience; it's covered with camel leather, which feels amazingly indulgent underfoot.

The sexiest bit is the suite's vast private terrace, where the glass-bottomed plunge pool, the scents and sounds shimmering up from the medina, the sun on your face and the sight of the snow-capped Atlas Mountains make for a heady ambience. From £435, B&B, with afternoon tea and champagne; 00 212 24 44 12 10, www.riadelfenn.com

7. VILLA 205 Maia, Seychelles—Picture that iconic love scene in From Here to Eternity, but with a toddler building a sandcastle in the background. Kind of kills the mood, doesn't it? To recreate that full-on, foam-thrashing fumble, you need some privacy, and this six-star villa comes with its very own seven-star Seychellois cove.

The sleek, Asian-inspired room is carved spectacularly into a Mahé cliff face, with 180-degree views of the azure Indian Ocean, and has the coolest infinity pool - but the pièce de résistance is the thatched alfresco sunken bath, which takes two. As dusk approaches, line the sides with tea lights and pour in an indecent amount of the room's obscenely expensive La Prairie bubble bath. Lying back, you won't be thinking of England. From £1,739, B&B; 00 248 390000, www.maia.com.sc

8. ROOM 20 Coeur des Alpes—If the soaring peak of the Matterhorn, bathed in morning sunshine, doesn't inspire you ... well, you probably need a different date. The penthouse suite at this cool little B&B - designed by local guru Heinz Julen - makes full use of uninterrupted views up the mountain, with double-height windows and an open-plan layout that allows you to sample it from every angle - including from the freestanding bath.

Book at least six months in advance, though - at £287 a night, this superb room is no more expensive than many regular doubles in Zermatt, and word is spreading ... From £287, B&B; 00 41 27 966 4080, www.coeurdesalpes.ch

9. SEIGNEURS D'ALBON Château de Bagnols—Number nine in the list and still no Rapunzel role-playing? Time to correct that with this gorgeous room, tucked away at the top of a tower in France's foremost chateau hotel. Strictly speaking, it's the bathroom (with freestanding bath) that's in the tower - and even more strictly speaking, you're going to have trouble letting your hair down through a 13th-century crossbow slit - but you can pretend.

Or just be content with a liaisons dangereuses fantasy, since we are in France. Beyond the thickly soundproofed walls of your deluxe room, you'll find a romantic Michelin-starred restaurant, cocktails on the moat walls and perfect, absolutely perfect rolling Beaujolais hills. Sexy in a classic way. From £430; 00 33 4 74 71 40 00, www.chateaudebagnols.co.uk

10. THE BOUDOIR Escape, Llandudno—How Anne Robinson would snigger; but, pound for pound, this place delivers way above its room rate in terms of passion-inducing panache. There's the handcrafted French rococo bed, aided and abetted by the dainty decoish mirrored bedside cabinets, a glass-drop chandelier, antiquey beaded lamps, gold metallic wallpaper and an array of fluffy and chiffon-ribboned scatter cushions.

It also has a flat-screen TV and DVD player, so you can snuggle down for a champagne movie session after a bracing walk along one of the UK's finest Victorian piers. Granted, there's no claw-footed, freestanding bath, but, as compensation, you get a Starck-esque shower and Aveda amenities. Escape might not satisfy the ginger winker, but the other Mrs Robinson would happily graduate in adult-education studies from here. From £99, B&B; 01492 877776, www.escapebandb.co.uk

Hotel Bathroom

A bathroom is a room that may have different functions depending on the culturalist context. In the most literal sense, the word bathroom means "a room with a bath". Because the traditional bathtubs have partly made way for modern showers, including steam showers, the more general definition is "a room where one bathes".

There can be just a *shower* (or *shower-bath*), just a *bath* (or *bathtub*) or both; and often both plumbing fixtures are combined in the bathtub. The room may also contain a sink (or *wash basin* or *hand basin*), a lavatory and a bidet.

In the United States, "bathroom" commonly means "a room containing a lavatory". In other countries this is usually called the "toilet" or alternatively "water closet" (WC), lavatory or "loo". The word "bathroom" is also used in the U.S. for a public toilet (the more formal U.S. term being "restroom").

Although it was not with hygiene in mind, the first records for the use of baths date back as far as 3000 B.C. At this time water had a strong religious value, being seen as a purifying element for both body and soul, and so it was not uncommon for people to be required to cleanse themselves before entering a sacred area. Baths are recorded as part of a village or town life throughout this period, with a split between steam baths in Europe and America and cold baths in Asia. Communal baths were erected in a distinctly separate area to the living quarters of the village, with a view to preventing evil spirits from entering the domestic quarters of a commune.

According to Teresi et al. (2002): The third millennium B.C. was the "Age of Cleanliness." Toilets and sewers were invented in several parts of the world, and Mohenjo-Daro circa 2800 B.C. had some of the most advanced, with lavatories built into the outer walls of houses. These were "Western-style" toilets made from bricks with wooden seats on top. They had vertical chutes, through which waste fell into street drains or cesspits. Sir Mortimer Wheeler, the director general of archaeology in India from 1944 to 1948, wrote, "The high quality of the sanitary arrangements could well be envied in many parts of the world today."

Nearly all of the hundreds of houses excavated had their own bathing rooms. Generally located on the ground floor, the bath was made of brick, sometimes with a surrounding curb to sit on. The water drained away through a hole in the floor, down chutes or pottery pipes in the walls, into the municipal drainage system. Even the fastidious Egyptians rarely had special bathrooms.

Not all ancient baths were in the style of the large pools that often come to mind when one imagines the Roman baths; the earliest surviving bathtub dates back to 1700 B.C, and hails from the Palace of Knossos in Crete. What is remarkable about this tub is not only the similarity with the baths of today, but also the way in which the plumbing works surrounding it differ so little from modern models.

A more advanced prehistoric (15th century BC and before) system of baths and plumbing is to be found in the excavated town of Akrotiri, on the Aegean island of Thera. There, alabaster tubs and other bath fittings were found, along with a sophisticated twin plumbing system to transport hot and cold water separately.

This was probably because of easy access to geothermic hot springs on this volcanic island. Both the Greeks and the Romans recognised the value of bathing as an important part of their lifestyles. Writers such as Homer had their heroes bathe in warm water so as to regain their strength; it is perhaps notable that the mother of Achilles bathed him in order to gain his invincibility. Palaces have been uncovered throughout Greece with areas that are dedicated to bathing, spaces with ceramic bathtubs, as well as sophisticated drainage systems.

The Roman attitudes towards bathing are well documented; they built large purpose-built thermal baths, marking not only an important social development, but also providing a public source of relaxation and rejuvenation. Here was a place where people could meet to discuss the matters of the day and enjoy entertainment. During this period there was a distinction between private and public baths, with many wealthy families having their own thermal baths in their houses.

Despite this they still made use of the public baths, showing the value that they had as a public institution. The strength of the Roman Empire was telling in this respect; imports from throughout the world allowed the Roman citizens to enjoy ointments, incense, combs, and mirrors.

Although some sources suggest that bathing declined following the collapse of the Roman Empire, this is not completely accurate. It was actually the Middle Ages that saw the beginning of soap production, proof that bathing was definitely not uncommon. It was only after the Renaissance that bathing declined; water was feared as a carrier of disease, and thus sweat baths and heavy perfumes were preferred.

In fact throughout the 16th, 17th, and 18th centuries, the use of public baths declined gradually in the west, and private spaces were favoured, thus laying the foundations for the bathroom, as it was to become, in the 20th century. However in Japan shared bathing in sento and onsen (spas) still exists; the latter being very popular.

Variations

A **shower room** or **shower-room** is a room that contains a shower cubicle (or shower stall), but no bathtub. In the United States, this would be called a *3/4 bathroom.*

En-suite

An en-suite bathroom or en-suite shower room (also en suite, ensuite and other variations) is a bathroom or shower room attached to and only accessible from a bedroom.

Family Bathroom

A family bathroom, in British estate agent terminology, is a full bathroom in a house where one or more bedrooms have en-suites.

Jack and Jill Bathroom

A Jack and Jill bathroom is a bathroom with two doors, accessible from two bedrooms.

Regional Differences

New Zealand

In New Zealand and other British Commonwealth countries it is common for a bathroom to *not* contain a lavatory; but with a separate 'toilet' next door (a very small room with only a toilet and perhaps a tiny hand washbasin).

Design Considerations

The design of a bathroom must account for the use of both hot and cold water, in significant quantities, for cleaning the human body. The water is also used for moving solid and liquid human waste to a sewer or septic tank. Water may be splashed on the walls and floor, and hot humid air may cause condensation on cold surfaces. From a decorating point of view the bathroom presents a challenge.

Ceiling, wall and floor materials and coverings should be impervious to water and readily and easily cleaned. The use of ceramic or glass, as well as smooth plastic materials, is common in bathrooms for their ease of cleaning. Such surfaces are often cold to the touch, however, and so water-resistant bath mats or even bathroom carpets may be used on the floor to make the room more comfortable. Alternatively, the floor may be heated, possibly by strategically placing heater conduits close to the surface.

Electrical appliances, such as lights, heaters, and heated towel rails, generally need to be installed as fixtures, with permanent connections rather than plugs and sockets. This minimizes the risk of electric shock. Ground-fault circuit interruptor electrical sockets can reduce the risk of electric shock, and are required for bathroom socket installation by electrical and building codes in the United States and Canada. In some countries, such as the United Kingdom, only special sockets suitable for electric shavers are permitted in bathrooms, and are labelled as such. UK Building Regulations also define what type of electrical light fittings (i.e. how water-/splash-proof) may be installed in the areas (zones) around and above baths, sinks and showers.

5

THE GROWTH STRATEGIES OF FOOD AND BEVERAGE INDUSTRY

U.S. food industry is the largest individual manufacturing sector of the economy. Its basic growth determinant is the underlying 1 percent per annum U.S. population growth. The share of personal consumption of expenditures for food and beverages has been dropping. Nevertheless, surviving food companies have demonstrated growth rates in revenues and returns to shareholders higher than the market as a whole. Growth has been achieved by a high rate of new product introductions, promotion methods to develop brand strengths, expansion into international markets, and by acquisitions and divestitures. Before 1980, a substantial portion of food company acquisitions were in non-food industries. During the 1980s, non-food divestitures returned food companies to their core food product lines with some exceptions. In general, the response of financial markets was positive to mergers and acquisitions that moved food companies closer to their core food activities.

This is a study of strategic growth in the food industry. The processed food and beverage industry is the largest individual manufacturing sector, with a value of industry shipments in 1993 of over $400 billion. M&A activity has been high for many decades. The industry provides rich case materials for testing propositions about strategies for growth. Our central aim is to relate performance among companies in the food industry to acquisition and divestiture strategies.

Economic Characteristics of the Food

Industry

The economic characteristics of the U.S. food industry raise important strategic issues. Its basic growth determinant is the underlying I percent per annum U.S. population growth to which the food industry is tied. Thus it is a 1 percent growth industry in a world in which firms strive for growth rates of 10 percent or more in order to attract high quality managerial capabilities and other critical resources. This is the challenge faced by food industry firms.

Consumer Spending Patterns

Shifts in consumer spending patterns have aggravated the food industry's ties to demographics. The U.S. population is aging and average household size is declining. Both trends negatively influence the food industry. For example, the share of personal consumption expenditures (PCE) for food and beverages dropped from 18 percent in 1982 to about 15 percent in 1993. Because of the pressure on real incomes, consumers have become more price sensitive; they have become "hard-nosed" bargain hunters.

Demand for Product Variety

Real growth rates in the lower value-added sectors, such as meat, poultry, and the fats and oils industry, have actually declined in recent years. A basic strategy to overcome these unfavorable influences is to shift to higher value-added products, such as frozen and canned fruits and vegetables, jellies, ice cream, and roasted nuts, for which growth has been at about a 2 percent real per annum rate. But such actions alone would not substantially lift the growth rate of food companies.

Consumers demand variety. A high rate of introduction of new products is required to maintain a firm's competitive position. But high growth rates for a product class rarely persist for more than five to ten years, and sharp reversals may occur. A study of growth in sixty-eight food and beverage classes reflects rapidly shifting consumer preferences with related price adjustments [Connor, 1988].

Promotion and Distribution

Because of the rapid rate of new product introductions, promotion and advertising are required to inform potential customers of their availability. As with other industries with high rates of product introduction, promotion and advertising expenditures are in the range of 25 to 35 percent of sales. The aim is to establish strong brand images. A strong brand requires attractive products plus substantial outlays on promotion.

Branded products give a firm a protected market position that erodes relatively quickly. Nevertheless, having a family of strong brands is a desirable foundation upon which a firm may build. Even a strong continued position in a given branded product area is not sufficient to enable a firm to maintain a high rate of growth. For example, Kellogg has had a continued strong position in a number of traditional cereal products such as corn flakes. Nevertheless, its market position in the ready-to-eat cereal segment of the food industry has eroded from 45 percent in the 1970s to 35 percent in 1995, while private labels have doubled their market share to 10 percent since 1988.

Strategy of Food Industry

The food industry is a complex, global collective of diverse businesses that together supply much of the food energy consumed by the world population. Only subsistence farmers, those who survive on what they grow, can be considered outside of the scope of the modern food industry.

It is challenging to find an inclusive way to cover all aspects of food production and sale. The Food Standards Agency, a government body in the UK, describes it thus:

"...the whole food industry – from farming and food production, packaging and distribution, to retail and catering."

The Economic Research Service of the USDA uses the term *food system* to describe the same thing:

"The U.S. food system is a complex network of farmers and the industries that link to them. Those links include makers of farm equipment and chemicals as well as firms that provide services to agribusinesses, such as providers of transportation and financial services. The system also includes the food marketing industries that link farms to consumers, and which include food and fiber processors, wholesalers, retailers, and foodservice establishments."

Industry Size

Processed food sales worldwide are approximately US$3.2 trillion (2004).

In the U.S., consumers spend approximately US$1 trillion annually on food, or nearly 10 percent of the Gross Domestic Product (GDP). Over 16.5 million people are employed in the food industry.

Agriculture

Agriculture is the process of producing food, feed, fiber and other desired products by the cultivation of certain plants and the raising of domesticated animals (livestock). The practice of agriculture is also known as "farming", while scientists, inventors and others devoted to improving farming methods and implements are also said to be engaged in agriculture. More people in the world are involved in agriculture as their primary economic activity than in any other, yet it only accounts for four percent of the world's Gross Domestic Product (GDP).

The food industry includes:

- Regulation: local, regional, national and international rules and regulations for food production and sale, including food quality and food safety, and industry lobbying activities
- Education: academic, vocational, consultancy
- Research and development: food technology
- Financial services insurance, credit
- Manufacturing: agrichemicals, seed, farm machinery and supplies, agricultural construction, etc.
- Agriculture: raising of crops and livestock, seafood
- Food processing: preparation of fresh products for market, manufacture of prepared food products
- Marketing: promotion of generic products (e.g. milk board), new products, public opinion, through advertising, packaging, public relations, etc.
- Wholesale and distribution: warehousing, transportation, logistics

Food Processing

Food processing is the methods and techniques used to transform raw ingredients into food for human consumption. Food processing takes clean, harvested or slaughtered and butchered components and uses them to produce marketable food products. There are several different ways in which food can be produced.

One Off Production

This method is used when customers make an order for something to be made to their own specifications, for example a wedding cake. The making of One Off Products could take days depending on how intricate the design is and also the ability of the chef making the product.

Batch Production

This method is used when the size of the market for a product is not clear, and where there is a range within a product line. A certain number of the same goods will be produced to make up a batch or run, for example at Gregg's Bakery they will bake a certain number of chicken bakes. This method involves estimating the amount of customers that will want to buy that product.

Mass Production

This method is used when there is a mass market for a large number of identical products, for example, chocolate bars, ready meals and canned food. The product passes from one stage of production to another along a production line.

Just In Time

This method of production is mainly used in sandwich bars such as Subway. All the components of the product are there and the customer chooses what they want in their product and it is made for them fresh in front of them.

Wholesale and Distribution

A vast global transportation network is required by the food industry in order to connect its numerous parts. These include suppliers, manufacturers, warehousing, retailers and the end consumers. There are also companies that add vitamins, minerals, and other necessary requirements during processing to make up for those lost during preparation.

Wholesale markets for fresh food products have tended to decline in importance in OECD countries as well as in Latin America and some Asian countries as a result of the growth of supermarkets, which procure directly from farmers or through preferred suppliers, rather than going through markets.

The constant and uninterrupted flow of product from distribution centers to store locations is a critical link in food industry operations. Distribution centers run more efficiently, throughput can be increased, costs can be lowered, and manpower better utilized if the proper steps are taken when setting up a material handling system in a warehouse.

Retail

With populations around the world concentrating in urban areas, food buying is increasingly removed from all aspects of food production. This is a relatively recent development, having taken place mainly over the last 50 years. The supermarket is the defining retail element of the food industry, where tens of thousands of products are gathered in one location, in continuous, year-round supply. Restaurants, Cafes, Bakeries and Mobile trucks are also ways consumers can purchase food.

Food preparation is another area where change in recent decades has been dramatic. Today, two food industry sectors are in apparent competition for the retail food dollar. The grocery industry sells fresh and largely raw products for consumers to use as ingredients in home cooking. The food service industry by contrast offers prepared food, either as finished products, or as partially prepared components for final "assembly".

Food Industry Technologies

Sophisticated technologies define modern food production. They include many areas. Agricultural machinery, originally led by the tractor, has practically eliminated human labor in many areas of production. Biotechnology is driving much change, in areas as diverse as agrochemicals, plant breeding and food processing. Many other areas of technology are also involved, to the point where it is hard to find an area that does not have a direct impact on the food industry. Computer technology is also a central force, with computer networks and specialized software providing the support infrastructure to allow global movement of the myriad components involved.

Marketing

As consumers grow increasingly removed from food production, the role of product creation, advertising, publicity become the primary vehicles for information about food. With processed food as the dominant category, marketers have almost infinite possibilities in product creation.

Media and Marketing

A key tool for FMCG marketing managers targeting the supermarket industry includes national titles like *The Grocer* in the U.K., *Checkout* in Ireland, *Progressive Grocer* in the U.S., and *Private Label Europe* for the entire of the European Union.it

Labour and Education

Until the last 100 years, agriculture was labor intensive. Farming was a common occupation. Food production flowed from millions of farms. Farmers, largely trained from generation to generation, carried on the family business. That situation has changed dramatically. In North America, over 50% of the population were farm families only a few decades ago; now, that figure is around 1-2%, and about 80% of the population lives in cities. The food industry as a complex whole requires an incredibly wide range of skills. Several hundred occupation types exist within the food industry.

Research and Development

Research in agricultural and food processing technologies happens in great part in university research environments. Projects are often funded by companies from the food industry. There is therefore a direct relationship between the academic and commercial sectors, as far as scientific research.

Prominent Food Companies

- Nestlé is the world's largest food and beverage company.
- PepsiCo is the largest U.S.-based food and beverage company.
- Unilever is an Anglo-Dutch company that owns many of the world's consumer product brands in foods and beverages.
- Kraft is apparently the world's second largest food company, following its acquisition of Cadbury in 2010.
- DuPont and Monsanto Company are the leading producers of pesticide, seeds, and other farming products.
- Both Archer Daniels Midland and Cargill process grain into animal feed and a diverse group of products. ADM also provides agricultural storage and transportation services, while Cargill operates a finance wing.
- Bunge is a global soybean exporter and is also involved in food processing, grain trading, and fertilizer.

- Dole Food Company is the world's largest fruit company. Chiquita Brands International, another U.S.-based fruit company, is the leading distributor of bananas in the United States. Sunkist Growers, Incorporated is a U.S.-based grower's cooperative.
- JBS S.A. is the world's largest processor and marketer of chicken, beef, and pork. Smithfield Foods is the world's largest pork processor and hog producer.
- Sysco Corporation, mainly catering to North America, is one of the world's largest food distributors.
- General Mills is the world's sixth biggest food manufacturing company.
- Grupo Bimbo is one of the most important baking companies in brand and trademark positioning, sales, and production volume around the world.

Food Packaging

Food packaging is packaging for food. It requires protection, tampering resistance, and special physical, chemical, or biological needs. It also shows the product that is labeled to show any nutrition information on the food being consumed.

Temperature recorders are used to monitor products shipped in a cold chain and to help validate the cold chain. Digital temperature data loggers measure and record the temperature history of food shipments. They sometimes have temperatures displayed on the indicator or have other output (lights, etc): The data from a shipment can be downloaded (cable, RFID, etc) to a computer for further analysis.

These help identify if there has been temperature abuse of products and can help determine the remaining shelf life. They can also help determine the time of temperature extremes during shipment so corrective measures can be taken. Radio Frequency Identification is applied to food packages for supply chain control and have shown a significant benefit in allowing food producers and retailers create full real time visibility of their supply chain.

Principles of food Packaging

The main general principle of food packaging is better containment, protection against physical, chemical, biological and environmental factors. To aid consumers in using products, communicate, educate about the ingredients, nutritional contents and the materials used to provide the protection.

Objectives

Packaging has several objectives:

- **Physical protection**—The food enclosed in the package may require protection from, among other things, shock, vibration, compression, temperature, etc.
- **Barrier protection**—A barrier from oxygen, water vapor, dust, etc., is often required. Permeation is a critical factor in design. Some packages contain desiccants or Oxygen absorbers to help extend shelf life. Modified atmospheres or controlled atmospheres are also maintained in some food packages. Keeping the contents clean, fresh, and safe for the intended shelf life is a primary function.
- **Containment or agglomeration**—Small items are typically grouped together in one package for reasons of efficiency. powders, and granular materials need containment.
- **Information transmission**—Packages and labels communicate how to use, transport, recycle, or dispose of the package or product. Some types of information are required by governments.

- **Marketing**—The packaging and labels can be used by marketers to encourage potential buyers to purchase the product. Package design has been an important and constantly evolving phenomenon for several decades. Marketing communications and graphic design are applied to the surface of the package and (in many cases) the point of sale display.
- **Security**—Packaging can play an important role in reducing the security risks of shipment. Packages can be made with improved tamper resistance to deter tampering and also can have tamper-evident features to help indicate tampering. Packages can be engineered to help reduce the risks of package pilferage: Some package constructions are more resistant to pilferage and some have pilfer indicating seals. Packages may include authentication seals to help indicate that the package and contents are not counterfeit. Packages also can include anti-theft devices, such as dye-packs, RFID tags, or electronic article surveillance tags, that can be activated or detected by devices at exit points and require specialized tools to deactivate. Using packaging in this way is a means of retail loss prevention.
- **Convenience**—Packages can have features which add convenience in distribution, handling, stacking, display, sale, opening, reclosing, use, and reuse.

Portion control—Single serving packaging has a precise amount of contents to control usage. Bulk commodities (such as salt) can be divided into packages that are a more suitable size for individual households. It also aids the control of inventory: selling sealed one-liter-bottles of milk, rather than having people bring their own bottles to fill themselves.

Food Packaging Types

The above materials are fashioned into different types of food packages and containers such as:

Packaging type	Type of container	Food examples
Aseptic processings	Primary	Liquid whole eggs
Plastic trays	Primary	Portion of fish
Bags	Primary	Potato chips
Boxes	Secondary	Box of Cola
Cans	Primary	Can of Tomato soup.
Cartons	Primary	Carton of eggs
Flexible packaging	Primary	Bagged salad
Pallets	Tertiary	A series of boxes on a single pallet used to transport from the manufacturing plant to a distribution center.
Wrappers	Tertiary	Used to wrap the boxes on the pallet for transport.

Primary packaging is the main package that holds the food that is being processed. Secondary packaging combines the primary packages into one box being made. Tertiary packaging combines all of the secondary packages into one pallet.

There are also special containers that combine different technologies for maximum durability:

- Bags-In-Boxes (used for soft drink syrup, other liquid products, and meat products)

- Wine box (used for wine)

Packaging Machines

A choice of packaging machinery includes technical capabilities, labor requirements, worker safety, maintainability, serviceability, reliability, ability to integrate into the packaging line, capital cost, floorspace, flexibility (change-over, materials, etc.), energy usage, quality of outgoing packages, qualifications (for food, phamaceuticals, etc.), throughput, efficiency, productivity, ergonomics, etc.

Packaging machines may be of the following general types:

- Blister, Skin and Vacuum Packaging Machines
- Capping, Over-Capping, Lidding, Closing, Seaming and Sealing Machines
- Cartoning machines
- Case and Tray Forming, Packing, Unpacking, Closing and Sealing Machines
- Check weighing machines
- Cleaning, Sterilizing, Cooling and Drying Machines
- Conveying, Accumulating and Related Machines
- Feeding, Orienting, Placing and Related Machines
- Filling Machines: handling liquid and powdered products
- Package Filling and Closing Machines
- Form, Fill and Seal Machines
- Inspecting, Detecting and Checkweighing Machines
- Palletizing, Depalletizing, Pallet Unitizing and Related Machines
- Product Identification: labelling, marking, etc.

- Wrapping Machines
- Converting Machines
- Other speciality machinery

Reducing Food Packaging

Reduced packaging and sustainable packaging are becoming more frequent. The motivations can be government regulations, consumer pressure, retailer pressure, and cost control. (Reduced packaging often saves packaging costs.)

In the UK, A Local Government Association survey produced by the British Market Research Bureau, compared a range of outlets to buy 29 common food items, found that small local retailers and market traders "produced less packaging and more that could be recycled than the larger supermarkets."

Trends in Food Packaging

Numerous reports industry associations agree that use of smart indicators will increase. There are a number of different indicators with different benefits for food producers, consumers and retailers.

Time-Temperature Indicators

Time-Temperature Indicators integrate the time and temperature experienced by the indicator and adjacent foods. Some use chemical reactions that result in a color change while others use the migration of a dye through a filter media. To the degree that these physical changes in the indicator match the degradation rate of the food, the indicator can help indicate probable food degradation.

Biodegradable Packaging

Plastic packaging being used is usually non-biodegradable due to possible interactions with the food.

Also, biodegradable polymers often require special composting conditions to properly degrade. Normal sealed landfill conditions do not promote biodegredation.

Biodegradable plastics includes biodegradable films and coatings synthesized from organic materials and microbial polymers. A biodegradable product has a unique characteristic in which microbes such as bacteria, fungi and algae can decompose the rugged polymer structure.

Food Fortification

Food fortification is the public health policy of adding micronutrients (essential trace elements and vitamins) to foodstuffs to ensure that minimum dietary requirements are met.

Simple diets based on staple foods with little variation are often deficient in certain nutrients, either because they are not present in sufficient amounts in the soil of a region, or because of the inherent inadequacy of the diet. Addition of micronutrients to staples and condiments can prevent large-scale deficiency diseases in these cases.

Several ranges of food supplements are recognised:

- Additives which repair a deficit to "normal" levels
- Additives which appear to enhance a food
- Supplements taken in addition to the normal diet

Many physicians today disagree with the premise that foodstuffs need supplementation , but accept that - for example - added calcium may provide benefit, or that adding folic acid may correct a nutritional deficiency especially in pregnant women.

On a more controversial level, but well founded in scientific basis , is the science of using foods and food supplements to achieve a defined health goal. A common example of this use of food supplements is the extent to which body builders will use amino acid mixtures, vitamins and phytochemicals to enhance natural hormone production, increase muscle and reduce fat.

Moving on from this reasonably accepted usage, there is increasing evidence for the use of food supplements in established medical conditions. This nutritional supplementation using foods as medicine (nutraceuticals) has been effectively used in treating disorders affecting the immune system up to and including cancers. This goes beyond the definition of "food supplement", but should be included for the sake of completeness.

There are several main groups of food supplements which can be considered:

- Vitamins and co-vitamins
- Essential minerals
- Essential fatty acids
- Essential amino acids
- Glyconutrients
- Phytonutrients
- Enzymes

Examples of Fortified Foods

Iodised salt has been used in the United States since before World War II.

Folic acid is added to flour in many industrialized countries, and has prevented a significant number of neural tube defects in infants. It is, however, not uniform in its application, with more intake of folic acid through fortified flour among those who were already receiving high amounts through their diet.

Niacin has been added to bread in the USA since 1938 (when voluntary addition started), a programme which substantially reduced the incidence of pellagra.

Vitamin D is added to a few foods (especially margarine).

Fluoride salts are added to water and toothpastes to prevent tooth decay. Water fluoridation is a controversial topic in some segments of the general public, although less so amongst established scientific bodies.

Calcium is frequently added to fruit juices, carbonated beverages and rice.

"Golden rice" is a variety of rice which has been genetically modified to produce beta carotene.

Alcoholic Beverage Industry in Europe

The alcoholic beverage industry in Europe is the source of a quarter of the world's alcohol and over half of the world's wine production. Trade is even more centered on Europe, with 70% of alcohol exports and just under half of the world's imports involving the European Union (EU). Although the majority of this trade is between EU countries, the trade in alcohol contributes around 9 billion euros to the goods account balance for the EU as a whole.

At least 1 in 6 tourists returns from trips abroad with alcoholic drinks, carrying an average of over 2 liters of pure alcohol per person in several countries. Europe also has a problem with illegal transport of alcohol; the European High Level Group on Fraud estimated that 1.5 billion euros were lost to alcohol fraud in 1996.

Alcohol excise duties in the EU countries amounted to 25 billion euros in 2001, excluding sales taxes and other taxes paid within the supply chain – although 1.5 billion euros is given back to the supply chain through the Common Agricultural Policy.

Alcohol is also associated with a number of jobs, including over 750,000 jobs in alcoholic beverage (mainly wine) production. Further jobs are also related to alcohol elsewhere in the supply chain, e.g. in pubs or shops.

Alcoholic Beverage

An alcoholic beverage is a drink containing ethanol, commonly known as alcohol. Alcoholic beverages are divided into three general classes: beers, wines, and spirits. They are legally consumed in most countries, and over 100 countries have laws regulating their production, sale, and consumption. In particular, such laws specify the minimum age at which a person may legally buy or drink them. This minimum age varies between 16 and 25 years, depending upon the country and the type of drink. Most nations set it at 18 years of age.

The production and consumption of alcohol occurs in most cultures of the world, from hunter-gatherer peoples to nation-states. Alcoholic beverages are often an important part of social events in these cultures. In many cultures, drinking plays a significant role in social interaction — mainly because of alcohol's neurological effects.

Alcohol is a psychoactive drug that has a depressant effect. A high blood alcohol content is usually considered to be legal drunkenness because it reduces attention and slows reaction speed. Alcohol can be addictive, and the state of addiction to alcohol is known as alcoholism.

Types

Alcoholic beverages that have a lower alcohol content (beer and wine) are produced by fermentation of sugar- or starch-containing plant material. Beverages of higher alcohol content (spirits) are produced by fermentation followed by distillation.

Beer

Beer is the world's oldest and most widely consumed alcoholic beverage and the third most popular drink overall after water and tea. It is produced by the brewing and fermentation of starches which are mainly derived from cereal grains — most commonly malted barley although wheat, maize (corn), and rice are also used. Alcoholic beverages which are distilled after fermentation, fermented from non-cereal sources such as grapes or honey, or fermented from un-malted cereal grain, are not classified as beer.

The two main types of beer are lager and ale. Ale is further classified into varieties such as pale ale, stout, and brown ale.

Most beer is flavored with hops, which add bitterness and act as a natural preservative. Other flavorings, such as fruits or herbs, may also be used. The alcoholic strength of beer is usually 4% to 6% alcohol by volume (ABV), but it may be less than 1% or more than 20%, and at least as high as 55%.

Beer is part of the drinking culture of various nations and has acquired social traditions such as beer festivals, cantus, pub culture, pub games, and pub crawling.

The basics of brewing beer are shared across national and cultural boundaries. The beer-brewing industry is global in scope, consisting of several dominant multinational companies and thousands of smaller producers, which range from regional breweries to microbreweries .

Wine

Wine is produced from grapes, and fruit wine is produced from fruits such as plums, cherries, or apples. Wine involves a longer (complete) fermentation process and a long aging process (months or years) that results in an alcohol content of 9%–16% ABV. Sparkling wine can be made by adding a small amount of sugar before bottling, which causes a secondary fermentation to occur in the bottle.

Spirits

Unsweetened, distilled, alcoholic beverages that have an alcohol content of at least 20% ABV are called *spirits.* Spirits are produced by the distillation of a fermented base product. Distilling concentrates the alcohol and eliminates some of the congeners.

Spirits can be added to wines to create *fortified wines,* such as port and sherry.

Alcohol Content of Beverages

The concentration of alcohol in a beverage is usually stated as the percentage of alcohol by volume (ABV) or as *proof.*

In the United States, *proof* is twice the percentage of alcohol by volume at 60 degrees Fahrenheit (e.g., 80 proof = 40% ABV). *Degrees proof* were formerly used in the United Kingdom, where 100 degrees proof was equivalent to 57.1% ABV. Historically, this was the most dilute spirit that would sustain the combustion of gunpowder.

Ordinary distillation cannot produce alcohol of more than 95.6% ABV (191.2 proof) because at that point alcohol is an azeotrope with water. A spirit which contains a very high level of alcohol and *does not contain any added flavoring* is commonly called a neutral spirit. Generally, any distilled alcoholic beverage of 170 proof or higher is considered to be a neutral spirit.

Most yeasts cannot reproduce when the concentration of alcohol is higher than about 18%, so that is the practical limit for the strength of fermented beverages such as wine, beer, and sake. Strains of yeast have been developed that can reproduce in solutions of up to 25% ABV.

Standard Drinks

A standard drink is a notional drink that contains a specified amount of pure alcohol. The standard drink is used in many countries to quantify alcohol intake. It is usually expressed as a measure of beer, wine, or spirits. One standard drink always contains the same amount of alcohol regardless of serving size or the type of alcoholic beverage.

The standard drink varies significantly from country to country. For example, it is 7.62 ml (6 grams) of alcohol in Austria, but in Japan it is 25 ml (19.75 grams).

In the United Kingdom, there is a system of units of alcohol which serves as a guideline for alcohol consumption. A single unit of alcohol is defined as 10 ml. The number of units present in a typical drink is printed on bottles. The system is intended as an aid to people who are regulating the amount of alcohol they drink; it is not used to determine serving sizes.

In the United States, the standard drink contains 0.6 US fluid ounces (18 ml) of alcohol. This is approximately the amount of alcohol in a 12-US-fluid-ounce (350 ml) glass of beer, a 5-US-fluid-ounce (150 ml) glass of wine, or a 1.5-US-fluid-ounce (44 ml) glass of a 40% ABV (80 proof) spirit.

Serving Sizes

In the United Kingdom, serving size in licensed premises is regulated under the Weights and Measures Act (1985). Spirits (gin, whisky, rum, and vodka) are sold in 25 ml or 35 ml quantities or multiples thereof. Beer is typically served in pints (568 ml), but is also served in half-pints or third-pints.

In the Republic of Ireland, serving size is 37.5 ml or multiples thereof. Beer is usually served in glasses of 400 or 500 ml, but may be as much as one liter. In the Netherlands and Belgium, standard servings are 250 and 500 ml for pilsner; 300 and 330 ml for ales.

Alcohol is a moderately good solvent for many fatty substances and essential oils. This attribute facilitates the use of flavoring and coloring compounds in alcoholic beverages, especially distilled beverages. Flavors may be naturally present in the beverage's base material. Beer and wine may be flavored before fermentation. Spirits may be flavored before, during, or after distillation.

Sometimes flavor is obtained by allowing the beverage to stand for months or years in oak barrels, usually American or French oak. A few brands of spirits have fruit or herbs inserted into the bottle at the time of bottling.

Liquor that contains 40%–50% ABV will catch fire if heated to about 80 °F (27 °C) and if an ignition source is applied to it. (This is called its flash point.) Beverages with lower concentrations of alcohol will also burn if sufficiently heated and an ignition source (such as an electric spark or a match) is applied to them. For example, the flash point of ordinary wine containing 12.5% alcohol is about 125 °F (52 °C).

Uses

In many countries, people drink alcoholic beverages at lunch and dinner. Studies have found that when food is eaten before drinking alcohol, alcohol absorption is reduced and the rate at which alcohol is eliminated from the blood is increased. The mechanism for the faster alcohol elimination appears to be unrelated to the type of food. The likely mechanism is food-induced increases in alcohol-metabolizing enzymes and liver blood flow.

At times and places of poor public sanitation (such as Medieval Europe), the consumption of alcoholic drinks was a way of avoiding water-borne diseases such as cholera. Small beer and faux wine, in particular, were used for this purpose. Although alcohol kills bacteria, its low concentration in these beverages would have had only a limited effect. More important was that the boiling of water (required for the brewing of beer) and the growth of yeast (required for fermentation of beer and wine) would tend to kill dangerous microorganisms.

The alcohol content of these beverages allowed them to be stored for months or years in simple wood or clay containers without spoiling. For this reason, they were commonly kept aboard sailing vessels as an important (or even the sole) source of hydration for the crew, especially during the long voyages of the early modern period.

In cold climates, potent alcoholic beverages such as vodka are popularly seen as a way to "warm up" the body, possibly because alcohol is a quickly absorbed source of food energy and because it dilates peripheral blood vessels (peripherovascular dilation). This is a misconception because the "warmth" is actually caused by a transfer of heat from the body's core to its extremities, where it is quickly lost to the environment. However, the perception alone may be welcomed when only comfort, rather than hypothermia, is a concern.

Nordic Countries

Two Nordic countries (Finland, and Norway) had a period of alcohol Prohibition in the early 20th century. This was the result of social democratic campaigning. Prohibition did not have popular support, and it resulted in large-scale smuggling.

In Sweden, prohibition was heavily discussed, but never introduced, replaced by strict rationing and later by more lax regulation, which included allowing alcohol to be sold on Saturdays.

Following the end of prohibition, government alcohol monopolies were established with detailed restrictions and high taxes. Some of these restrictions have since been lifted. For example, supermarkets in Finland are allowed to sell only fermented beverages with an alcohol content up to 4.7% ABV, but Alko, the government monopoly, is allowed to sell wine and spirits. This is also the case with the Swedish Systembolaget and the Norwegian Vinmonopolet.

United States

In the United States, there was an attempt from 1920 to 1933 to eliminate the drinking of alcoholic beverages by means of a national prohibition of their manufacture and sale. This period became known as the *Prohibition era.* During this time, the 18th Amendment to the Constitution of the United States made the manufacture, sale, and transportation of alcoholic beverages illegal throughout the United States.

Prohibition led to the unintended consequence of causing widespread disrespect for the law, as many people procured alcoholic beverages from illegal sources. In this way, a lucrative business was created for illegal producers and sellers of alcohol, which led to the development of organized crime. As a result, Prohibition became extremely unpopular, which ultimately led to the repeal of the 18th Amendment in 1933.

Prior to national Prohibition, beginning in the late 19th century, many states and localities had enacted Prohibition within their jurisdictions. After the repeal of the 18th Amendment, some localities (known as dry counties) continued to ban the sale of alcohol.

6

THE GROWTH STRATEGIES OF FOOD SERVICE AND RESTAURANT INDUSTRY

Foodservice (US English) or catering industry (British English) defines those businesses, institutions, and companies responsible for any meal prepared outside the home. This industry includes restaurants, school and hospital cafeterias, catering operations, and many other formats.

The companies that supply foodservice operators are called foodservice distributors. Foodservice distributors sell goods like small wares (kitchen utensils) and foods. Some companies manufacture products in both consumer and foodservice versions. The consumer version usually comes in individual-sized packages with elaborate label design for retail sale. The foodservice version is packaged in a much larger industrial size and often lacks the colorful label designs of the consumer version.

Foodservice sales to restaurants and institutions are estimated to be approximately $400 billion, about equal with consumer sales of foods through grocery outlets. Major foodservice providers include Aramark, Brinker International, Compass Group, the Crown Group, Darden

Restaurants, Sysco, McLane Company, US Foodservice and 3663 First for Foodservice.

The foodservice industry is one of the largest employers in the United States. Over 805,360 people are currently working as servers and managers alone. 59% of these workers are under the age of 30, and over 66% hold only a high school diploma or less.

Counter Service

Counter service is a form of service in restaurants, pubs, and bars where food or drinks are ordered at the counter. Counter service is also called "bar service" in the case of pubs and bars where the counter is also called the bar. Counter service is compared with table service where service is provided at the table. With counter service, the customer generally pays before consuming the food or drink. Some fast food restaurants offer only counter service while table service is the common form in most restaurants. For pubs and bars, bar service is the norm in the United Kingdom and the Republic of Ireland whereas table service is the norm in the United States and Continental Europe.

Table Service

Table service is food service served to the customer's table by waiters and waitressess, also known as "servers". Table service is the norm in most restaurants, while for some fast food restaurants counter service is the common form. For pubs and bars, table service is the norm in the United States whereas counter service is the norm in the United Kingdom. With table service, the customer generally pays at the end of meal. Various methods of table service can be provided..

Gueridon Service

Gueridon service is a form of food service provided by restaurants to their guests. This type of service encompasses preparing food (primarily salads, main dishes such as beef stroganoff, or desserts) in direct view of the guests, using a "Gueridon". A gueridon typically consists of a trolley that is well equipped to prepare, cook and serve the food to the guest. There will be a gas hob, chopping board, cutlery drawer, cold store (depending on the trolley type) and general working area.

Bottle Service

Bottle service is a feature of many upscale bars and nightclubs where patrons may purchase entire bottles of liquor for their personal consumption.

The purchase of bottle service typically includes a reserved table for the patron's party and mixers of the patron's choice. Bottle service can include the service of a VIP host, who will ensure that patrons have sufficient mixers and will often make drinks using the patrons' liquor bottle and mixers. The purchase of bottle service sometimes results in cover charge being waived for the purchaser's party, and often allows patrons to bypass entrance lines.

The cost of a bottle at such a bar or club is usually extremely marked up, often by 2000% or more (20×), and can account for a significant portion of an establishment's revenue.

Early forms of bottle service existed in World War II era Japan, where unfinished bottles would be stored. In its modern form, an early example was in 1988 at the Paris nightclub *Les Bains Douches*, bottle service was introduced to deal with an excess of customer demand. An early, inexpensive form of bottle service ($90, compared with $6 drinks) was established at the *Tunnel* in 1993 (by Jeffrey Jah and Mark Baker). The modern form of bottle service was pioneered in 1995 by Michael Ault at *Spy Bar* and in 1996, *Chaos* ($175 for a bottle of Stolichnaya vodka), with the express goal of creating a "barrier to entry", rather than of increasing liquor sales. The concept later spread to other American cities, notably Miami and Las Vegas in the early 2000s.

Restaurant

A restaurant prepares and serves food, drink and dessert to customers in return for money. Meals are generally served and eaten on premises, but many restaurants also offer take-out and food delivery services. Restaurants vary greatly in appearance and offerings, including a wide variety of the main chef's cuisines and service models.

While inns and taverns were known from antiquity, these were establishments aimed at travellers, and in general locals would rarely eat there. Modern restaurants, as businesses dedicated to the serving of food, and where specific dishes are ordered by the guest and generally prepared according to this order, emerged only in 18th-century Europe, although similar establishments had also developed in China.

A restaurant owner is called a *restaurateur*; both words derive from the French verb *restaurer*, meaning "to restore". Professional artisans of cooking are called chefs, while preparation staff and line cooks prepare food items in a more systematic and less artistic fashion.

Food catering establishments which may be described as restaurants were known since the 11th century in Kaifeng, China's northern capital during the first half of the Song Dynasty (960–1279). With a population of over 1,000,000 people, a culture of hospitality and a paper currency, Kaifeng was ripe for the development of restaurants. Probably growing out of the tea houses and taverns that catered to travellers, Kaifeng's restaurants blossomed into an industry catering to locals as well as people from other regions of China. Stephen H. West argues that there is a direct correlation between the growth of the restaurant businesses and institutions of theatrical stage drama, gambling and prostitution which served the burgeoning merchant middle class during the Song Dynasty.

Restaurants catered to different styles of cuisine, price brackets, and religious requirements. Even within a single restaurant much choice was available, and people ordered the entree they wanted from written menus. An account from 1275 writes of Hangzhou, the capital city for the last half of the dynasty:

"The people of Hangzhou are very difficult to please. Hundreds of orders are given on all sides: this person wants something hot, another something cold, a third something tepid, a fourth something chilled; one wants cooked food, another raw, another chooses roast, another grill".

The restaurants in Hangzhou also catered to many northern Chinese who had fled south from Kaifeng during the Jurchen invasion of the 1120s, while it is also known that many restaurants were run by families formerly from Kaifeng.

Types of Restaurants

Restaurants range from unpretentious lunching or dining places catering to people working nearby, with simple food served in simple settings at low prices, to expensive establishments serving refined food and wines in a formal setting. In the former case, customers usually wear casual clothing. In the latter case, depending on culture and local traditions, customers might wear semi-casual, semi-formal, or even in rare cases formal wear.

Typically, customers sit at tables, their orders are taken by a waiter, who brings the food when it is ready, and the customers pay the bill before leaving. In finer restaurants there will be a host or hostess or even a maître d'hôtel to welcome customers and to seat them. Other staff waiting on customers include busboys and sommeliers.

Restaurants often specialize in certain types of food or present a certain unifying, and often entertaining, theme. For example, there are seafood restaurants, vegetarian restaurants or ethnic restaurants. Generally speaking, restaurants selling food characteristic of the local culture are simply called restaurants, while restaurants selling food of foreign cultural origin are called accordingly,

Restaurant Regulations

Depending on local customs and the establishment, restaurants may or may not serve alcohol. Restaurants are often prohibited from selling alcohol without a meal by alcohol sale laws; such sale is considered to be activity for bars, which are meant to have more severe restrictions. Some restaurants are licensed to serve alcohol ("fully licensed"), and/or permit customers to "bring your own" alcohol (BYO / BYOB). In some places restaurant licenses may restrict service to beer, or wine and beer.

Restaurant Guides

Restaurant guides review restaurants, often ranking them or providing information for consumer decisions (type of food, handicap accessibility, facilities, etc). In 12th century Hangzhou (mentioned above as the location of the first restaurant), signs could often be found posted in the city square listing the restaurants in the area and local customer's opinions of the quality of their food.

This was an occasion for bribery and even violence. One of the most famous contemporary guides, in Western Europe, is the Michelin series of guides which accord from 1 to 3 stars to restaurants they perceive to be of high culinary merit. Restaurants with stars in the Michelin guide are formal, expensive establishments; in general the more stars awarded, the higher the prices. The main competitor to the Michelin guide in Europe is the guidebook series published by Gault Millau. Unlike the Michelin guide which takes the restaurant décor and service into consideration with its rating, Gault Millau only judges the quality of the food. Its ratings are on a scale of 1 to 20, with 20 being the highest.

In the United States, the Forbes Travel Guide (previously the Mobil travel guides) and the AAA rate restaurants on a similar 1 to 5 star (Forbes) or diamond (AAA) scale. Three, four, and five star/diamond ratings are roughly equivalent to the Michelin one, two, and three star ratings while one and two star ratings typically indicate more casual places to eat. In 2005, Michelin released a New York City guide, its first for the United States. The popular Zagat Survey compiles individuals' comments about restaurants but does not pass an "official" critical assessment. In the United Kingdom, diners can freely express their opinion on where they eat in The people's UK restaurant guide. In the United States Gault Millau is published as the *Gayot* guide, after founder Andre Gayot. Its restaurant ratings use the same 20 point system, and are all published online.

The Good Food Guide, published by the Fairfax Newspaper Group in Australia, is the Australian guide listing the best places to eat. Chefs Hats are awarded for outstanding restaurants and range from one hat through three hats. The Good Food Guide also incorporates guides to bars, cafes and providers. *The Good Restaurant Guide* is another Australian restaurant guide that has reviews on the restaurants as experienced by the public and provides information on locations and contact details. Any member of the public can submit a review.

Nearly all major American newspapers employ food critics and publish online dining guides for the cities they serve. A few papers maintain a reputation for thorough and thoughtful review of restaurants to the standard of the good published guides, but others provide more of a listings service.

More recently Internet sites have started up that publish both food critic reviews and popular reviews by the general public. Their major competition comes from bloggers, particularly publishers of food blogs, also called foodies. These writers and publishers represent the common dining aficionado rather than the gourmet, and thus do not provide "official" reviews, but nonetheless are capable of garnering large, loyal followings.

United States

As of 2006, there are approximately 215,000 full-service restaurants in the United States, accounting for $298 billion, and approximately 250,000 limited-service (fast food) restaurants, accounting for $260 billion.

One study of new restaurants in Cleveland, Ohio found that 1 in 4 changed ownership or went out of business after one year, and 6 out of 10 did so after three years. (Not all changes in ownership are indicative of financial failure.) The three-year failure rate for franchises was nearly the same.

Canada

There are 86,915 commercial foodservice units in Canada, or 26.4 units per 10,000 Canadians. By segment, there are:

- 38,797 full-service restaurants
- 34,629 limited-service restaurants
- 741 contract and social caterers
- 6,749 drinking places

Fully 63% of restaurants in Canada are independent brands. Chain restaurants account for the remaining 37%, and many of these are locally owned and operated franchises.

Culinary Art

Culinary art is the art of preparing and cooking foods. The word "culinary" is defined as something related to, or connected with, cooking. A culinarion is a person working in the culinary arts. A culinarian working in restaurants is commonly known as a cook or a chef. Culinary artists are responsible for skillfully preparing meals that are as pleasing to the palate as to the eye.

Increasingly they are required to have a knowledge of the science of food and an understanding of diet and nutrition. They work primarily in restaurants, fast food chain store franchises, delicatessens, hospitals and other institutions. Kitchen conditions vary depending on the type of business, restaurant, nursing home, etc.

Careers in Culinary Arts

Related Careers

Below is a list of the wide variety of culinary arts occupations.

- Consulting and Design Specialists - Work with restaurant owners in developing menus, the layout and design of dining rooms, and service protocols.
- Dining Room Service- Manage a restaurant, cafeterias, clubs, etc. Diplomas and degree programs are offered in restaurant management by colleges around the world.
- Food and Beverage Controller - Purchase and source ingredients in large hotels as well as manage the stores and stock control.
- Entrepreneurship- Deepen and invest in businesses, such as bakeries, restaurants, or specialty foods (such as (chocolates, cheese, etc.).
- Food and Beverage Managers - Manage all food and beverage outlets in hotels and other large establishments.
- Food Stylists and Photographers - Work with magazines, books, catalogs and other media to make food visually appealing.

- Food Writers and Food Critics - Communicate with the public on food trends, chefs and restaurants though newspapers, magazines, blogs, and books. Notables in this field include Julia Child, Craig Claiborne and James Beard.
- Research and Development Kitchens - Develop new products for commercial manufacturers and may also work in test kitchens for publications, restaurant chains, grocery chains, or others.
- Sales - Introduce chefs and business owners to new products and equipment relevant to food production and service.
- Instructors - Teach aspects of culinary arts in high school, vocational schools, colleges, recreational programs, and for specialty businesses (for example, the professional and recreational courses in baking at King Arthur Flour).

Occupational Outlook

The occupation outlook for chefs, restaurant managers, dietitians, and nutritionists is fairly good, with "as fast as the average" growth. Increasingly a college education with formal qualifications is required for success in this field. It has been recorded that 54% of all culinary art professionals are female.

Restaurant Management

Restaurant management is the profession of managing a restaurant. Associate, bachelor, and graduate degree programs are offered in restaurant management by community colleges, junior colleges, and some universities in the United States.

Floor Management

'Floor management' includes managing staff who give services to customers and allocate the duties of opening and closing restaurant. The manager is responsible for making sure his or her staff is following the service standards and health and safety regulations. The manager is the most important person in the front-of-the-house environment, since it is up to him or her to motivate the staff and give them job satisfaction. The manager also looks after and guides the personal well-being of the staff, since it makes the work force stronger and more profitable.

Kitchen Management

'Kitchen management' includes the managing staff working in the kitchen, especially the head chef. The kitchen is the most important part of the business and the main reason customers patronize the restaurant. Managing the kitchen staff heips to control food quality. As most commercial kitchens are a closed environment, the staff may become bored or tired from the work. Without proper management, this often results in an inconsistent food product.

Kitchen management involves most importantly, cost control and budgeting. Meeting KPI's are a must for a restaurant to survive. Head chefs must instill and teach money management to apprentices. This is as important as teaching the art and skills of cookery.

Administration

'Administration' includes stock controlling, scheduling rotations, budgeting the labor costs, balancing cost and profit according to seasonality, surveying and hiring staff, and maintenance of the commercial kitchen equipment.

Franchising

Franchising is the practice of using another firm's successful business model. The word 'franchise' is of anglo-French derivation - from *franc-* meaning free, and is used both as a noun and as a (transitive) verb. For the franchisor, the franchise is an alternative to building 'chain stores' to *distribute* goods and avoid investment and liability over a chain. The franchisor's success is the success of the franchisees. The franchisee is said to have a greater incentive than a direct employee because he or she has a direct stake in the business.

However, except in the US, and now in China (2007) where there are explicit Federal (and in the US, State) laws covering franchise, most of the world recognizes 'franchise' but rarely makes legal provisions for it. Only Australia, various provinces within Canada, France and Brazil have significant Disclosure laws but Brazil regulates franchises more closely.

Where there is no specific law, franchise is considered a distribution system, whose laws apply, with the trademark (of the franchise system) covered by specific covenants.

Businesses for which franchising works best have the following characteristics:

- Businesses with a good track record of profitability.
- Businesses which are easily duplicated.

As practiced in retailing, franchising offers franchisees the advantage of starting up quickly based on a proven trademark, and the tooling and infrastructure as opposed to developing them.

Although there are franchises around products – Chanel and other cosmetics, to name the prominent – by and large, the franchises revolve around *service* firms. At the sub-$80,000 level, they are, by far, the largest number of franchises. Some franchises are available for a few thousand dollars.

The following US-listing tabulates the early 2010 ranking of major franchises along with the number of sub-franchisees (or partners) from data available for 2004. It will also be seen from the names of the franchise that the US is a leader in franchising innovations, a position it has held since the 1930s when it took the major form of fast-food restaurants, food inns and, slightly later, the motels during the first depression. Franchising is a business model used in more than 70 industries that generates more than $1 trillion in U.S. sales annually (2001 study). Franchised businesses operated 767,483 establishments in the United States in 2001, counting both establishments owned by franchisees and those owned by franchisors:

1. Subway (Sandwiches and Salads | *Startup costs* $84,300 – $258,300 (22000 partners worldwide in 2004).
2. McDonald's | *Startup costs* in 2010, $995,900 – $1,842,700 (37,300 partners in 2010)
3. 7-Eleven Inc. (Convenience Stores) | *Startup Costs* $40,500- 775,300 in 2010,(28,200 partners in 2004)
4. Hampton Inns & Suites (Midprice Hotels) | *Startup costs* $3,716,000 – $15,148,800 in 2010
5. Great Clips (Hair Salons) | *Startup Costs* $109,000 - $203,000 in 2010
6. H&R Block (Tax Preparation and e-Filing) | *Startup Costs* $26,427 - $84,094 (11,200 partners in 2004)
7. Dunkin Donuts | *Startup Costs* $537,750 - $1,765,300 in 2010
8. Jani-King (Commercial Cleaning | *Startup Costs* $11,400 - $35,050, (11,000 partners worldwide in 2004)
9. Servo-Pro (Insurance and Disaster Restoration and Cleaning) | *Startup Costs* $102,250 - $161,150 in 2010
10. MiniMarkets (Convenience Store and Gas Station) | *Startup Costs* $1,835,823 - $7,615,065 in 2010

The midi-franchises like restaurants, gasoline stations, trucking stations which involve substantial investment and require all the attention of a business.

There are also the large franchises - hotels, spas, hospitals, etc. - which are discussed further in Technological Alliances.

Two important payments are made to a franchisor: (a) a royalty for the trade-mark and (b) reimbursement for the training and advisory services given to the franchisee. These two fees may be combined in a single 'management' fee. A fee for "Disclosure" is separate and is always a "front-end fee".

A franchise usually lasts for a fixed time period (broken down into shorter periods, which each require *renewal*), and serves a specific "territory" or area surrounding its location. One franchisee may manage several such locations. Agreements typically last from five to thirty years, with premature cancellations or terminations of most contracts bearing serious consequences for franchisees. A franchise is merely a temporary business investment, involving renting or leasing an opportunity, not buying a business for the purpose of ownership. It is classified as a wasting asset due to the finite term of the license.

Although franchisor revenues and profit may be listed in a franchise disclosure document (FDD), no laws require the estimate of franchisee *profitability*, which depends on how intensively the franchisee 'works' the franchise. Therefore, franchisor fees are always based on 'gross revenue from sales' and not on profits realized. See Remuneration.

Various tangibles and intangibles such as national or international advertising, training, and other support services are *commonly* made available by the franchisor.

Franchise brokers help franchisors find appropriate franchisees. There are also main 'master franchisors' who obtain the rights to sub-franchise in a territory.

According to the International Franchise Association approximately 4% of all businesses in the United States are franchisee-worked.

It should be recognized that franchising is one of the only means available to access venture investment capital *without the need to give up control* of the operation of the chain and build a distribution system for their services. After the brand and formula are carefully designed,and properly executed, franchisors are able to sell franchises and expand rapidly across countries and continents using the capital and resources of their 'franchisees' while reducing risk.

Franchisor rules imposed by the franchising authority are usually very strict and important in the US and most countries need to study them to help the small or start-up franchisee in their countries to protect them. Besides the trademark, there are proprietary service marks which may be copyright - and corresponding regulations.

Obligations of the Parties

Each party to a franchise has several interests to protect. The franchisor is most involved in securing protection for his trademark, *controlling* the business concept and securing his know-how. This requires the franchisee to carry out the services for which the trademark has been made prominent or famous. There is a great deal of standardization proposed. The place of service has to carry the franchisor's signs, logos and trademark in a prominent place. The uniforms worn by the staff of the franchisee have to be of a particular shade and colour. The service has to be in accordance to the pattern followed by the franchisor in his successful operations. Thus, for the franchisee he is not in full control of the business as he would be in retailing.

A service can be successful by buying equipment and supplies from the franchisor or those recommended by the franchisor if they are not over-priced. A coffee brew, for example, can be readily identified by the trademark when its raw materials come from a particular supplier. If the franchisor *requires* purchase from his stores, it *may* come under anti-trust legislation or equivalent laws of other countries. So too the purchase of uniforms of personnel, signs, etc. But it also applies to *sites* of franchise if they are owned or controlled by the franchisor.

The franchisee must carefully negotiate the license. They, along with the franchisor must develop a marketing plan or business plan. The fees must be fully disclosed and there should not be any hidden fees. The start-up and costs and working capital must be known before taking the license. There must be assurance that additional licensees not crowd the "territory" if the franchise is worked to plan. The franchisee must be seen as an independent merchant. He must be protected by the franchisor from any trademark infringement by third-parties. A franchise attorney is required to assist the franchisee during negotiations.

Most often the training period - the costs of which are in great part covered by the initial fee - is too short to operate complicated equipment and the franchisee has to learn on his own from Manuals. The training period must be adequate but in low-cost franchises it would be considered expensive. Many frachisors have set up corporate universities to train staff online. This is in addition to literature and sales documents and reach by email.

Also, franchise agreements carry no guarantees or warranties and the franchisee has little or no recourse to legal intervention in the event of a dispute. Franchise contracts tend to be unilateral contracts in favor of the franchisor; they are generally protected from lawsuits from their franchisee *because of the non-negotiable contracts that require franchisees to acknowledge, in effect, that they are buying the franchise knowing that there is risk, and that they have not been promised success or profits by the franchisor*. Contracts are renewable at their sole option. Most franchisors make franchisees sign agreements waiving their rights under federal and state law, and in some cases allowing the franchisor to choose where and under what law any dispute would be litigated.

Australia

In Australia, franchising is regulated by the "Franchising Code of Conduct", a mandatory code of conduct made under the Trade Practices Act 1974.

The Code requires franchisors to produce a disclosure document which must be given to a prospective franchisee at least 14 days before the franchise agreement is entered into.

The Code also regulates the content of franchise agreements, for example in relation to marketing funds, a cooling-off period, termination and the resolution of disputes by mediation.

The federal government is currently considering recommended changes to the Code of Conduct contained in the report, "Opportunity not Opportunism: Improving conduct in Australian Franchising" tabled by a Parliamentary inquiry into franchising on 4 December 2008.

Some experts have warned that any push to increase regulation of the franchising sector, could make it a less attractive means of doing business.

Brazil

In 2008, there were about 1,013 franchises with more than 62,500 outlets, making it one of the largest countries in the world in terms of number of units. Around 11 percent of this total are foreign-based franchisors.

The Brazilian Franchise Law (Law No. 8955 of December 15, 1994) defines the franchise as a system in which the franchisor *licenses* the franchisee, for a payment, the right to use a trademark/ patent along with the right to distribute products or services on an exclusive or semi-exclusive basis.

The "Franchise Offer Circular" or disclosure document is mandatory before execution of agreement and is valid for all of Brazilian territory. Failure to disclose voids the agreement with refunds and serious damages.

The Franchise Law does not distinguish between Brazilian and foreign franchisors. The National Institute of Industrial Property (INPI) is the registering authority. Indispensable documents are the Statement of Delivery (of disclosure documentation) and Certification of Recording (INPI). The latter is necessary for payments. All sums amounts may not be convertible into foreign currency. Certification may also mean compliance with Brazil's antitrust legislation.

Parties to international franchising may decide to adopt the English language for the document, as long as the Brazilian party knows English fluently and expressly acknowledges that fact, to avoid translation (but it follows). The Registration accomplishes three things:

- It make the agreement effective against third parties
- Permits the remittance of payments
- Qualifies the franchisee for tax deductions

China

China has the most franchises in the world but the scale of their operations is relatively small. Each system in China has an average of 43 outlets, compared to more than 540 in the United States. Together, there are 2600 brands in some 200,000 retail markets. KFC was the most significant foreign entry in 1987 and is widespread Many franchises are in fact joint-ventures, as at their forming the franchise law was not explicit. For example, McDonalds is a joint venture. Pizza Hut, TGIF, Wal-mart, Starbucks followed a little later. But total franchising is only 3% of retail trade which is hungry for foreign franchise growth.

The year 2005 saw the birth of an updated franchise law, "Measures for the Administration of Commercial Franchise". Previous legislation (1997) made no specific inclusion of foreign investors. Today the Franchise Law is much clearer by virtue of the 2007 law, a revision of the 2005 Law.

The laws are applicable if there are transactions involving a trademark combined with payments with many obligations on the franchiser. The Law comprises 42 Articles and 8 chapters.

Among the franchisor obligations are:

- the FIE (foreign-invested enterprise) franchisor must obtain registration by the regulator
- The franchisor (or its subsidiary) *must have operated at least operated two company-owned franchises in China (revised to* anywhere*)for more than 12 months ("the two-store, one-year" rule)*
- the franchisor must disclosure *any* information requested by the franchisee
- cross-border franchising, with some caveats, is possible (2007 law).

The franchisor must meet a list of requirements for registration, among which are:

- the standard franchise agreement, working Manual and working capital requirements,
- track-record of operations, and ample ability to supply materials, and
- the ability to train the Chinese personnel and provide them
- long-term operational guidance.
- the franchise agreement must have a minimum three-year term

Among other provisions is:

- the franchisor will be liable for certain actions of its suppliers
- monetary and other penalties apply for infractions of the regulations.

The Disclosure has to take place 20 days in advance. It has to contain:

- Details of the franchisor's experience in the franchised business with scope of business
- identification of the franchisor's principal officers
- litigation of the franchisor during the past five years
- full details about all franchise fees
- the amount of a franchisee's initial investment
- a list of the goods or services the franchisor can supply, and the terms of supply
- the training franchisees will receive
- information about the trademarks,including registration, usage, and litigation
- demonstration of the franchisor's capabilities to provide training and guidance
- statistics about existing units, including number, locations, and operational results, and the percentage of franchises that have been terminated; and
- an audited financial report and tax information (for an unspecified period of time)

Other elements of this legislation are:

- the franchisee's confidentiality obligations continue indefinitely after termination or expiration of the franchise agreement

- if the franchisee has paid a deposit to the franchisor, it must be onded on termination of the franchise agreement; and, upon termination, the franchisee is prohibited from continuing to use the franchisor's marks.

Europe

Franchising has grown rapidly in Europe in recent years, but the industry is largely unregulated. Unlike the United States, the European Union has not adopted a uniform franchise disclosure policy. Only five countries in Europe have adopted pre-sale disclosure obligations. They are France (1989), Spain (1996), Romania (1997), Italy (2004) and Belgium (2005).

The Code of Ethics of the European Franchising Federation is self-enforced in seventeen European states where their national franchise associations are members of EFF members, and UNIDROIT.

All formal disclosure countries are require to give "Contract Summaries" to be furnished, highlighting:

- the object of the contract
- the rights and obligations of the parties
- the financial conditions
- the term of the contract

Legal consultation is a must to enter and finalize the agreement(s) as it in all regions. Most often one of the principal tasks in Europe is to find retail space, not so significant a factor in the US. This is where the franchise broker, or the master franchisor, plays a significant role. Cultural factors are also significant as the populations tend to be homogeneous.

France

France is one of Europe's largest market. Similar to the United States, it has a long history of franchising, dating back to 1930s. Growth came in the 70s. The market is considered tough for outside franchisors because of its cultural angularities; yet, McDonald's and Century 21 are found everywhere. There are some 30 US Firms involved in franchising.

There are no government agencies regulating franchises. The Loi Doubin of 1989 was the first European Franchise Disclosure law. Combined with Decree No. 91-337, they regulate disclosure, although the decree also applies to any person who provides to another person a corporate name, trademark or trade name other business arrangements. The law applies to "exclusive or quasi-exclusive territory".

In brief, the disclosure document must be delivered at least 20 days before the execution of the agreement or any payments are made.

The specific and important disclosures to be made are :

1. the date of the founding of the franchisor's enterprise and a summary of its business history and all information necessary to assess the business experience of the franchisor including bankers,
2. a description of the local market for the goods or services,
3. franchisor's financial statements for the previous two years,
4. a list of all other franchisees currently in the network,
5. all franchisees who have left the network during the preceding year, whether by termination or non-renewal, and
6. the conditions for renewal, assignment, termination and the scope of exclusivity.

Initially, there was some uncertainty whether any breach of the provisions of the Doubin law would enable the Franchisee to walk away from the contract. However, the Supreme Court (Cour de cassation) eventually ruled that agreements should only be annulled where missing or incorrect information affected the decision of the franchisee to enter into the Agreement. The burden of proof is on the franchisee.

Dispute Settlement features are only incorporated in some European countries. By not being rigorous, franchising is encouraged.

Italy

Under the Italian law franchise is defined as an arrangement between two financially independent parties where a franchisee is granted, in exchange for consideration, the right to market goods and services under trademarks. In addition, articles which dictate the form and content of the franchise agreement and define the documents that must be made available 30 days prior to execution. The franchisor must disclose:

1. a summary of the franchise activities and operations,
2. a list of franchisees currently operating in the franchise system in Italy,
3. year-by-year details of the changes in the number of franchisees for the previous three years in Italy,
4. a summary of any court or arbitral proceedings in Italy related to the franchise system, and
5. if requested by the franchisee, copies of franchisor's balance sheets for the previous three years, or, since start-up if period is shorter.

Spain

Legal definition of Franchising in Spain is the activity in which an undertaking, the franchisor, grants to another party, the franchisee, for a specific market and in exchange of an economic financial compensation (either direct, indirect or both) the right to exploit an own system to commercialize products or services already exploited by the franchisor with enough success and experience.

The Spanish Retail Trading Act regulates franchising. The contents of the Franchise must include, at least:

- The use of a common name or brand or any other intellectual property right and a uniform presentation of the premises or the transport means included in the agreement.
- The communication by the franchisor to the franchise of certain technical knowledge or a substantial and singular know-how that has to be owned by the franchisor, and
- A technical or commercial assistance or both, provided by the franchisor to the franchisee during the agreement, without prejudice of any supervision faculty that the parties could freely agree in the contract.

In Spain, the franchisor submits the Disclosure information 20 days prior to the signature of the Agreement or prior to any payment made by the franchisee to the franchisor. Franchisors should disclose to the potential franchisee some specific information in writing. This information has to be true and not misleading and includes:

- ' Identification of the franchisor;
- Justification of ownership or license for use of any trademark or similar sign and judicial claims affecting them as well as the duration of the license;
- General description of the sector in which the franchise operates;
- Experience of the franchisor;
- Contents and characteristics of the franchise and its exploitation;

- Structure and extension of the network in Spain;
- Essential elements of the franchise agreement.

Franchisors (with some exceptions) should be registered in the Franchisors' Register and provide some information. According to the regulation in force in 2010 this obligation has to be done within the term of three months since the starting of its activities in Spain.

UK

In the United Kingdom, there are no franchise-specific laws; franchises are subject to the same laws that govern other businesses. For example, franchise agreements are produced under regular contract law and do not have to conform to any further legislation or guidelines. There is some self-regulation through the British Franchise Association (BFA).

However there are many franchise businesses which do not become members, and many businesses that refer to themselves as franchisors do not conform to these rules. There are several people and organisations in the industry calling for the creation of a framework to help reduce the number of "cowboy" franchises and help the industry clean up its image.

On 22 May 2007, hearings were held in the UK Parliament concerning citizen initiated petitions for special regulation of franchising by the government of the UK due to losses of citizens who had invested in franchises. The Minister of Industry, Margaret Hodge, conducted hearings but resisted any government regulation of franchising with the advice that government regulation of franchising might lull the public into a false sense of security. The Minister of Industry indicated that if due diligence were performed by the investors and the banks, the current laws governing business contracts in the UK offered sufficient protection for the public and the banks.

India

Franchising of goods and services, foreign to India, is in its infancy. The first International Exhibition was only held in 2009. India is, however, one of the biggest franchising markets because of its large middle-class of 300 million who are not reticent on spending and because the population is entrepreneurial in character. In a highly diversified society, McDonalds is a success story despite its fare differing from the rest of the world.

So far, franchise agreements are covered under two standard commercial laws: the Contract Act 1872 and the Specific Relief Act 1963, which provide for both specific enforcement of covenants in a contract and remedies in the form of damages for breach of contract.

Kazakhstan

In Kazakhstan franchise turnover for 2010 is 1 billion US$ dollars per year. Kazakhstan is the leader in Central Asia in the franchising market. There is a special law on the franchising of 2002, there are about 300 franchise systems and franchises near the 2000 outlets Kazakhstan franchise began with the emergence of a factory "Coca-Cola", opened to sublicense Turkish licensor of the same brand. The plant was built in 1994. Other brands that are also present in Kazakhstan through the franchise system include Pepsi, Hilton, Marriott, Intercontinental, Pizza Hut etc.

New Zealand

New Zealand is served by over 350 franchise systems .... giving it the highest proportion of franchises per capita in the world. There is no separate law covering franchises, so franchises are covered by normal commercial law. However, the self-regulatory Code of Practice introduced in 1996 by the Franchise Association of New Zealand contains many provisions similar to those of the Australian Franchising Code of Practice legislation.

Russia

In Russia, under chapter 54 of the Civil Code (passed 1996), franchise agreements are invalid unless written and registered, and franchisors cannot set standards or limits on the prices of the franchisee's goods. Enforcement of laws and resolution of contractual disputes is a problem: Dunkin' Donuts chose to terminate its contract with Russian franchisees that were selling vodka and meat patties contrary to their contracts, rather than pursue legal remedies.

U.S.

Isaac Singer, in the 1850s, who made improvements to an existing model of a sewing machine, was among the first franchising efforts in the United States, followed later by Coca-Cola, Western Union, etc. and agreements between automobile manufacturers and dealers.

Modern franchising came to prominence with the rise of franchise-based food service establishments. In 1932, Howard Deering Johnson established the first modern restaurant franchise based on his successful Quincy, Massachusetts Howard Johnson's restaurant founded in the late 1920s. The idea was to let independent operators use the same name, food, supplies, logo and even building design in exchange for a fee.

The growth in franchises picked up steam in the 1930s when such chains as Howard Johnson's started franchising motels. The 1950s saw a boom of franchise chains in conjunction with the development of the U.S. Interstate Highway System.

In the U.S. the (FTC) Federal Trade Commission requires that the franchisee be furnished with a Franchise Disclosure Document (FDD) by the franchisor at least fourteen days before money changes hands or a franchise agreement is signed. The final agreement is always a negotiated document setting forth fees and other terms. Whereas elements of the disclosure may be available from third parties only that provided by the franshisor can be depended upon.

The U.S. Franchise Disclosure Document (FDD) is very lengthy (300-700 pp +) and detailed , and generally provides audited financial statements of the franchisor in a particular format, although audited financial statements may not be required under some circumstances, such as where a franchisor is new. It will include data on the names, addresses and telephone numbers of the franchisees in the licensed territory (who may be contacted and consulted before negotiations), estimate of total franchise revenues and franchisor profitability.

The States may require the FDD to contain specific requirements but the requirements in the State disclosure documents must be in compliance with the Federal Rule that governs federal regulatory policy. There is no private right of action of action under the FTC Rule for franchisor violation of the rule but fifteen or more of the States have passed statutes that provide this right of action to franchisees when fraud can be proven under these special statutes. The majority of franchisors have inserted mandatory arbitration clauses into their agreements with their franchisees, in some of which the U.S. Supreme Court has dealt with.

There is no federal registry of franchises or any federal filing requirements for information. States are the primary collectors of data on franchising companies, and enforce laws and regulations regarding their presence and their spread in their jurisdictions.

Where the franchisor has many partners, the agreement may take the shape of a business format franchise - an agreement that is identical foı all franchisees.

Social Franchises

In recent years, the idea of franchising has been picked up by the social enterprise sector, which hopes to simplify and expedite the process of setting up new businesses. A number of business ideas, such as soap making, wholefood retailing, aquarium maintenance, and hotel operation, have been identified as suitable for adoption by social firms employing disabled and disadvantaged people.

The most successful example is probably the CAP Markets, a steadily growing chain of some 50 neighborhood supermarkets in Germany. Other examples are the St. Mary's Place Hotel in Edinburgh and the Hotel Tritone in Trieste.

Social franchising also refers to a technique used by governments and aid donors to provide essential clinical health services in the developing world.

Event Franchising

Event franchising is the duplication of public events in other geographical areas, while retaining the original brand (logo), mission, concept and format of the event. As in classic franchising, event franchising is built on precisely copying successful events. Good example of event franchising is the World Economic Forum, or just Davos forum which has regional event franchisees in China, Latin America etc. Likewise, the alter-globalist World Social Forum has launched many national events. When The Music Stops is an example of an events franchise in the UK, in this case, running speed dating and singles events.

Waiting Staff

Waiting staff, wait staff, or waitstaff are those who work at a restaurant or a bar attending customers — supplying them with food and drink as requested. Traditionally, a male waiting tables is called a "waiter" and a female a "waitress" with the gender-neutral version being a "server". Other gender-neutral versions include using *"waiter"* indiscriminately for males and females, *"waitperson"*, or the Americanism *"waitron"*, which was coined in the 1980s.

Waiting on tables is (along with nursing and teaching) part of the service sector, and among the most common occupations in the United States. The Bureau of Labor Statistics estimates that, as of May 2008, there were over 2.2 million persons employed as servers in the U.S. Many servers are required by their employers to wear a uniform.

Duties of Waiting Staff

The duties of waiting staff include preparing tables for a meal, taking customers' orders, serving drinks and food, and cleaning up before, after and during servings in a restaurant. Silver service staff are specially trained to serve at banquets or high-end restaurants. They follow specific rules of service and it is a skilled job.

They generally wear black and white with a long, white apron (extending from the waist to ankle). The head server is in charge of the waiting staff, and is also frequently responsible for assigning seating. The functions of a head server can overlap to some degree with that of the maître d'hôtel. Some restaurants employ busboys or busgirls, increasingly referred to as bussers, to clear dirty dishes, set tables, and otherwise assist the waiting staff.

Tipping

In the United States, United Kingdom, Canada, many other Western countries and parts of the Middle East, it is customary for customers to pay a tip to a server after a meal, with a possible range from 15% to 30% depending on the level and quality of service. In some situations, a tip or "service charge" will be included on the restaurant bill in the U.S. Also called a gratuity, a "service charge" will be automatically applied for situations where the restaurant management imposes this to ensure that the servers working in such situations earn their usual tip income.

Such service charges are usually around 18%; an additional voluntary tip is sometimes given. There is some debate in the U.S. whether a "minimum tip" exists as a convention; some argue that 15% or 20% is a minimum tip or that it is extremely rude to not leave at least $1, even if the service was not up to standard. However, some people also believe that a "minimum tip" is a way for employers to shift the responsibility of paying employee wages onto the customer. These issues are regional, cultural, and very subjective.

In Germany and other Western countries, where minimum wages exist for servers and where tipping is not culturally entrenched, most tips take the form of rounding up to the nearest whole or half denomination of currency when the server is cashing a party out at their table. In the United Kingdom it is common practice to tip 10% of the cost of the meal.

By contrast, servers in Japan refuse tips because it isn't a Japanese custom.

Tipping is not customary in Asia, Australia and New Zealand and is not factored into wages of staff, however tips may be appreciated. This is especially the case if the customer or party has been unusually difficult or has left a mess - parents of small children, for example, may leave a small tip. In these countries, tips are often placed into a Tip Jar and pooled rather than being kept by individual servers. This money is usually then spent on things that directly benefit staff - it may be used to maintain staff facilities or to fund events such as Christmas parties, for example.

In Taiwan and Hong Kong, a 10% service fee is often added to meals in middle-to-upscale restaurants. However, this fee does not go to the waitstaff - but is simply a surcharge that is added to the price of the meal.

Where tipping is common, it may be encouraged as a social convention, but on occasion may actually be vehemently enforced by the restaurant.

Cafeteria

A cafeteria is a type of food service location in which there is little or no waiting staff table service, whether a restaurant or within an institution such as a large office building or school; a school dining location is also referred to as a dining hall or canteen (in UK English). Cafeterias are different from coffeehouses, although that is the Spanish meaning of the English word.

Instead of table service, there are food-serving counters/stalls, either in a line or allowing arbitrary walking paths. Customers take the food they require as they walk along, placing it on a tray. In addition, there are often stations where customers order food and wait while it is prepared, particularly for items such as hamburgers or tacos which must be served hot and can be quickly prepared.

Alternatively, the patron is given a number and the item is brought to their table. Sometimes, for some food items and drinks, customers collect an empty container, pay at the check-out, and fill the container after the check-out. Free second servings are often allowed under this system. For legal purposes (and the consumption patterns of customers), this system is rarely or never used for alcoholic beverages in the USA.

Customers are either charged a flat rate for admission (as in a buffet), or pay at the check-out for each item. Some self-service cafeterias charge by the weight of items on a patron's plate.

As cafeterias require few employees, they are often found within a larger institution, catering to the clientele of that institution. For example, schools, colleges and their residence halls, department stores, hospitals, museums, military bases, prisons, and office buildings often have cafeterias.

At one time, upscale cafeteria-style restaurants dominated the culture of the Southern United States, and to a lesser extent the Midwest. There were several prominent chains of them: Bickford's, Morrison's Cafeteria, Piccadilly Cafeteria, S&W Cafeteria, Apple House, K&W, Britling, Wyatt's Cafeteria, and Blue Boar among them. Currently two midwest chains still exist, Sloppy Jo's Luchroom and Manny's, both located in Illinois. There were also a number of smaller chains, usually in and around a single city.

These institutions, with the exception of K&W, went into a decline in the 1960s with the rise of fast food and were largely finished off in the 1980s by the rise of "casual dining". A few chains — notably Luby's and Piccadilly Cafeterias (which took over the Morrison's chain), continue to fill some of the gap left by the decline of the older chains. Many of the smaller Midwestern chains, such as MCL Cafeterias centered around Indianapolis, are still very much in business.

The world's largest non-military cafeteria is in the Brody Complex at Michigan State University. Perhaps the first self-service restaurant (not necessarily cafeteria) in the United States was the Exchange Buffet in New York City, opened September 4, 1885, which catered to an exclusively male clientele. Food was purchased at a counter, and patrons ate standing up. This represents the predecessor of two formats: the cafeteria, described below, and the automat.

During the 1893 World's Columbian Exposition in Chicago, an entrepreneur named John Kruger built an American version of the smörgåsbords he had seen while traveling in Sweden. Emphasizing the simplicity and light fare, he called it the "Cafeteria" - Spanish for "coffee shop". The exposition attracted over 27 million visitors (half the US population at the time) in six months, and it was initially through Kruger's operation that America first heard the term and experienced the self-service dining format.

Meanwhile, in everyday, hometown America, the chain of Childs Restaurants was quickly growing from about 10 locations in New York City (in 1890), to hundreds across the United States and Canada (by 1920). Childs is credited with the critical innovation of adding trays and a "tray line" to the self-service format, which they introduced in 1898 at their 130 Broadway location. Childs did not change its format of sit-down dining, however. This was soon the standard design for most Childs Restaurants - and many imitators - from coast-to-coast, and ultimately the dominant design for cafeterias.

It has also been said that the "cafeteria craze started in May 1905, when a woman named Helen Mosher opened a humble downtown L.A. restaurant where people chose their food at a long counter and carried their own trays to their tables." California does have a long and rich history in the cafeteria format - most notably the many Boos Brothers Cafeterias, and also Clifton's and Schaber's. However, the facts do not warrant the "wellspring" characterization that some have ascribed to the region. The earliest cafeterias in California were opened at least 12 years after Kruger's Cafeteria, and Childs already had several dozen locations scattered around the country. Finally, Horn & Hardart, an automat format chain (only slightly different from the cafeteria), was also well established in the mid-Atlantic region before 1900.

Between 1960 and 1980, the popularity of cafeteria format restaurants was gradually overcome by the emergence of the fast food restaurant and fast casual restaurant formats.

Other Names

A cafeteria in a U.S. military installation is known as a chow hall, a mess hall, a galley, mess decks or, more formally, a dining facility, whereas in common British Armed Forces parlance, it is known as a cookhouse or mess. Students in the USA often refer to cafeterias as lunchrooms, though breakfast as well as lunch is often eaten there. Cafeterias serving university dormitories are sometimes called dining halls or dining commons. A food court is a type of cafeteria found in many shopping malls and airports featuring multiple food vendors or concessions, although a food court could equally be styled as a type of restaurant as well, being more aligned with public, rather than institutionalised, dining.

Some monasteries, boarding schools and older universities refer to their cafeteria as a **refectory**. Modern-day British cathedrals and abbeys, notably in the Church of England, often use the phrase **refectory** to describe a cafeteria open to the public. Historically, the refectory was generally only used by monks and priests. For example, although the original 800-year-old refectory at Gloucester Cathedral (the stage setting for dining scenes in the Harry Potter movies) is now mostly used as a choir practice area, the relatively modern 300-year-old extension, now used as a cafeteria by staff and public alike, is today referred to as the **refectory**.

A cafeteria located in a television studio is often called a commissary. NBC's commissary, The Hungry Peacock, was often joked about by Johnny Carson on The Tonight Show.

College Cafeteria

A college cafeteria is a term in the United States that denotes a cafeteria that is designed to serve college students at the university. In the UK the word *refectory* is often used. Also see the different meanings of the word college around the Anglosphere. These cafeterias can be a part of a residence hall or in a separate building. Many of these colleges employ their own students to work in the cafeteria.

The amount of meals served to students varies from school to school, but is normally around 20 meals per week.

Like normal cafeterias, a person will have a tray to select the food that they want, but instead of paying money, they pay beforehand by purchasing a meal plan.

The method of payment for college cafeterias is commonly in the form of a meal plan, whereby the patron pays a certain amount at the start of the semester and the details of the plan are stored on a computer system. Student ID cards are then used to access the meal plan. A meal plan is not necessary to eat at a college cafeteria however. Meal plans can vary widely in their details to best fit the needs of the students. Typically, the college tracks the student's usage of their plan by counting either the number of pre-defined meal servings, points, dollars, or number of buffet dinners. The plan may give the student a certain number of any of the above per week or semester and they may or may not roll over to the next week or semester.

Many schools offer several different options for using their meal plans. The main cafeteria is usually where most of the meal plan is used but smaller cafeterias, cafés, restaurants, bars, or even fast food chains located on campus may accept meal plans. A college cafeteria system often has a virtual monopoly on the students due to an isolated location or a requirement that residence contracts include a full meal plan. It is not uncommon for the entire food service operation to be outsourced to a managed services company such as Aramark, Sodexo and Compass Group (under the Scolarest name in the United Kingdom).

7

THE GROWTH STRATEGIES OF HOSPITALITY DESIGN

Hotel design is the discipline concerned with the creation of an environment in which guests can be welcomed and provided with facilities for rest, relaxation and respite from their travels or workaday cares in return for payment to their host. As such the designer is providing the hotelier with the tools to do his job. By value Hotel Design may only cost 15% of the budget for creating an hotel but it is said it can leverage up to 70% of the revenue by the creation of an attractive interior experience.

The discipline of Hotel Design is rooted in traditions of hospitality to travellers dating back to the first movements of early man. From the formalised travels of the court entourage and their expectations of the highest levels of hospitality to the humble journeying of ordinary trades' people the development of specialist buildings to meet their need has been seen in many cultures.

Examples range from the European Inn to guest palaces across Asia, from monasteries offering refuge to spare bedrooms let in ordinary houses. Often the development of such refuges was driven by their location – on river crossings, at major trading posts or in locations lending themselves to defence or domination of the local population, such as forts or castles.

Hotel Design today is a sophisticated discipline involving specialist architects, environmental and structural engineers, interior designers and skilled contractors and suppliers. The interior of an hotel may be the refurbishment of an existing building already used for the purpose, the conversion of a building previously used for another purpose or the construction of specialist buildings as an hotel but all need careful design to function effectively, as well as a good location.

Hotel design is essentially a marriage between the client brief and the designer vision. Hotel buildings have a clear specialist range of functions from restaurants to bedrooms, the operations of which must not interfere with each other through factors such as noise or the movement of people. Hotels are usually designed from the inside out to ensure the practical working and relationship of the parts in the most economical manner.

Cultural Influences

Hotel designers bring to their work their own cultural mores and need to understand the culture in which the hotel will operate if working outside their native environment. With the internationalisation of travellers the links with local traditions in many hotel designs have been weakened and 'International' has become a style in its own right, often denoting the bland and inoffensive.

This in turn has caused a reaction in many operators and guests who have sought out hotels with a vernacular local traditional style or created hotels where the design has been more linked to modernist stylistic tendencies of elites, the latter characterised by the boutique hotel. Stylistic influences of modern design are wide and shared through television and the web leading to a wide range of diverse stylistic exercises in hotel interiors from 'grunge' to 'classical'.

Yet the design of such buildings has become more focussed so the 'rules' governing their functionality have become more defined leading to the development of specialist knowledge in an expert cadre of hotel designers. Such knowledge ranges from the mundane, such as the appropriate height for bed head light switches to the more specialist, such as the right layout for a kitchen or the sightlines from reception to enable control and protection of entry to rooms.

The pace of change has, as in most areas of modern life, speeded up with the development of innovative technology, which also affects such design yet whether 'International', 'grunge', 'boutique' or 'urban' such design rules need to be applied in all hotels.

The parameters for success appear immutable. The Hotel still has to provide a welcome and an environment that supports the comfort of the guest, the provision or respite, rest and relaxation from the demands of a noisy and increasingly crowded society.

Interior Design

Interior design is a multi–faceted profession in which creative and technical solutions are applied within a structure to achieve a built interior environment.

The interior design process follows a systematic and coordinated methodology, including research, analysis, and integration of knowledge into the creative process, whereby the needs and resources of the client are satisfied to produce an interior space that fulfills the project goals.

Working Conditions

There are a wide range of working conditions and employment opportunities within interior design. Large and tiny corporations often hire interior designers as employees on regular working hours. Designers for smaller firms usually work on a contract or per-job basis. Self-employed designers, which make up 26% of interior designers, usually work the most hours.

Interior designers often work under stress to meet deadlines, stay on budget, and meet clients' needs. In some cases, licensed professionals review the work and sign it before submitting the design for approval by clients or construction permisioning.

The need for licensed review and signature varies by locality, relevant legislation, and scope of work. Their work can involve significant travel to visit different locations, however with technology development, the process of contacting clients and communicating design alternatives has become easier and requires less travel.

Earnings

Interior design earnings vary based on employer, number of years with experience, and the reputation of the individual. For residential projects, self-employed interior designers usually earn a per-hour fee plus a percentage of the total cost of furniture, lighting, artwork, and other design elements. For commercial projects, they may charge per-hour fees, or a flat fee for the whole project.

The median annual earning for wage and salary interior designers, in the year 2006, was $42,260. The middle 50% earned between $31,830 and $57,230. The lowest 10 percent earned less than $24,270, and the highest 10 percent earned more than $78,760. For example, if a person opens a business and decides to specialize in furniture design and flooring, they will get only clients focusing on these topics rather than a variety of every type of issue that comes with designing a home.

Interior Styles

A style, or theme, is a consistent idea used throughout a room to create a feeling of completeness. Styles are not to be confused with design concepts, or the higher-level party, which involve a deeper understanding of the architectural context, the socio-cultural and the programmatic requirements of the client. These themes often follow period styles. Examples of this are Louis XV, Louis XVI, Victorian, Islamic, Feng Shui, International, Mid-Century Modern, Minimalist, English Georgian, Gothic, Indian Mughal, Art Deco, and many more.

The evolution of interior decoration themes has now grown to include themes not necessarily consistent with a specific period style allowing the mixing of pieces from different periods. Each element should contribute to form, function, or both and maintain a consistent standard of quality and combine to create the desired design.

A designer develops a home architecture and interior design for a customer that has a style and theme that the prospective owner likes and mentally connects to. For the last 10 years, decorators, designers, and architects have been re-discovering the unique furniture that was developed post-war of the 1950s and the 1960s from new material that were developed for military applications. Some of the trendsetters include Charles and Ray Eames, Knoll and Herman Miller. Themes in home design are usually not overused, but serves as a guideline for designing.

On Television

Interior decoration (which is not to be confused with interior design, as noted above) has become the subject of television shows. In the United Kingdom (UK), popular interior decorating programs include *60 Minute Makeover* (ITV), *Changing Rooms* (BBC) and *Selling Houses* (Channel 4). Famous interior designers whose work is featured in these programs include Linda Barker and Laurence Llewelyn-Bowen. In the United States, the TLC Network aired a popular program called *Trading Spaces*, a show based on the UK program *Changing Rooms*.

In Canada, popular shows include Divine Design with Candice Olsen and Design Inc., featuring Sarah Richardson. In addition, both Home & Garden Television (*HGTV*) and the Discovery Home networks also televise many programs about interior design and decorating, featuring the works of a variety of interior designers, decorators and home improvement experts in a myriad of projects.

Fictional interior decorators include the Sugarbaker sisters on *Designing Women* and Grace Adler on *Will & Grace*. There is also another show called *Home MADE*. There are two teams and two houses and whoever has the designed and made the worst room, according to the judges, is eliminated.

Another show on the Style Network, hosted by Niecy Nash, is *Clean House* where they re-do messy homes into themed rooms that the clients would like. Other shows include *Design on a Dime*, *Designed to Sell* and *The Decorating Adventures of Ambrose Price*. The show called *Design Star* has become more popular through the 5 seasons that have already aired. The winners of this show end up getting their own TV shows, of which are *Color Splash* hosted by David Bromstad, *Myles of Style* hosted by Kim Myles, *Paint-Over!* hosted by Jennifer Bertrand, *The Antonio Treatment* hosted by Antonio Ballatore, and finally *Secrets from a Stylist* hosted by Emily Henderson.

Interior Decorators

Other early interior decorators:

- Elsie de Wolfe
- Syrie Maugham
- Sybil Colefax
- Dorothy Draper
- Pierre François Léonard Fontaine

Many of the most famous designers and decorators during the 20th Century had no formal training. Sister

Parish,Robert Denning and Vincent Fourcade, Kerry Joyce, Kelly Wearstler, Stéphane Boudin, Georges Geffroy, Emilio Terry, Carlos de Beistegui, Nina Petronzio, Lorenzo Mongiardino, David Nightingale Hicks and many others were trend-setting innovators in the worlds of design and decoration.

Interior Stylist

Advises and prepares construction documents consisting of plans, elevations, details and specifications to illustrate various elements of the design concept, including the non-structural and/or non-seismic partition layouts, power and communications locations, acoustic plans, lighting designs, furniture layouts and materials and finishes.

Architecture

A wider definition may comprise all design activity, from the macro-level (urban design, landscape architecture) to the micro-level (construction details and furniture). Architecture is both the process and product of planning, designing and constructing form, space and ambience that reflect functional, technical, social, and aesthetic considerations. It requires the creative manipulation and coordination of material, technology, light and shadow.

Architecture also encompasses the pragmatic aspects of realizing buildings and structures, including scheduling, cost estimating and construction administration. As documentation produced by architects, typically drawings, plans and technical specifications, architecture defines the structure and/or behavior of a building or any other kind of system that is to be or has been constructed.

Architectural works are often perceived as cultural and political symbols and as works of art. Historical civilizations are often identified with their surviving architectural achievements.

Architecture sometimes refers to the activity of designing any kind of system and the term is common in the information technology world.

Architects plan, design and review the construction of buildings and structures for the use of people. Architects also coordinate and integrate engineering design, which has as its primary objective the creative manipulation of materials and forms using mathematical and scientific principles.

Architecture can mean:

- The art and science of designing and erecting buildings and other physical structures.
- The practice of an architect, where architecture means to offer or render professional services in connection with the design and construction of a building, or group of buildings and the space within the site surrounding the buildings, that have as their principal purpose human occupancy or use.
- A general term to describe buildings and other structures.
- A style and method of design and construction of buildings and other physical structures.

The earliest surviving written work on the subject of architecture is *De architectura*, by the Roman architect Vitruvius in the early 1st century CE. According to Vitruvius, a good building should satisfy the three principles of *firmitas, utilitas, venustas*, which translate roughly as -

- Durability - it should stand up robustly and remain in good condition.
- Utility - it should be useful and function well for the people using it
- Beauty - it should delight people and raise their spirits.

According to Vitruvius, the architect should strive to fulfill each of these three attributes as well as possible. Leone Battista Alberti, who elaborates on the ideas of Vitruvius in his treatise, De Re Aedificatoria, saw beauty primarily as a matter of proportion, although ornament also played a part. For Alberti, the rules of proportion were those that governed the idealised human figure, the Golden mean. The most important aspect of beauty was therefore an inherent part of an object, rather than something applied superficially; and was based on universal, recognisable truths. The notion of style in the arts was not developed until the 16th century, with the writing of Vasari. The treatises, by the 18th century, had been translated into Italian, French, Spanish and English.

In the early nineteenth century, Augustus Welby Northmore Pugin wrote *Contrasts* (1836) that, as the titled suggested, contrasted the modern, industrial world, which he disparaged, with an idealized image of neo-medieval world. Gothic architecture, Pugin believed, was the only "true Christian form of architecture."

The 19th century English art critic, John Ruskin, in his *Seven Lamps of Architecture*, published 1849, was much narrower in his view of what constituted architecture. Architecture was the "art which so disposes and adorns the edifices raised by men ... that the sight of them" contributes "to his mental health, power, and pleasure".

For Ruskin, the aesthetic was of overriding significance. His work goes on to state that a building is not truly a work of architecture unless it is in some way "adorned". For Ruskin, a well-constructed, well-proportioned, functional building needed string courses or rustication, at the very least.

On the difference between the ideals of "architecture" and mere "construction", the renowned 20th C. architect Le Corbusier wrote: "You employ stone, wood, and concrete, and with these materials you build houses and palaces: that is construction. Ingenuity is at work. But suddenly you touch my heart, you do me good. I am happy and I say: This is beautiful. That is Architecture".

Modern Concepts of Architecture

The great 19th century architect of skyscrapers, Louis Sullivan, promoted an overriding precept to architectural design: "Form follows function".

While the notion that structural and aesthetic considerations should be entirely subject to functionality was met with both popularity and skepticism, it had the effect of introducing the concept of "function" in place of Vitruvius' "utility". "Function" came to be seen as encompassing all criteria of the use, perception and enjoyment of a building, not only practical but also aesthetic, psychological and cultural.

Nunzia Rondanini stated, "Through its aesthetic dimension architecture goes beyond the functional aspects that it has in common with other human sciences. Through its own particular way of expressing values, architecture can stimulate and influence social life without presuming that, in and of itself, it will promote social development.'

To restrict the meaning of (architectural) formalism to art for art's sake is not only reactionary; it can also be a purposeless quest for perfection or originality which degrades form into a mere instrumentality".

Among the philosophies that have influenced modern architects and their approach to building design are rationalism, empiricism, structuralism, poststructuralism, and phenomenology.

In the late 20th century a new concept was added to those included in the compass of both structure and function, the consideration of sustainability. To satisfy the contemporary ethos a building should be constructed in a manner which is environmentally friendly in terms of the production of its materials, its impact upon the natural and built environment of its surrounding area and the demands that it makes upon non-sustainable power sources for heating, cooling, water and waste management and lighting.

History

Origins and Vernacular Architecture

Building first evolved out of the dynamics between needs (shelter, security, worship, etc.) and means (available building materials and attendant skills). As human cultures developed and knowledge began to be formalized through oral traditions and practices, building became a craft, and "architecture" is the name given to the most highly formalized and respected versions of that craft.

It is widely assumed that architectural success was the product of a process of trial and error, with progressively less trial and more replication as the results of the process proved increasingly satisfactory.

What is termed vernacular architecture continues to be produced in many parts of the world. Indeed, vernacular buildings make up most of the built world that people experience every day. Early human settlements were mostly rural. Due to a surplus in production the economy began to expand resulting in urbanization thus creating urban areas which grew and evolved very rapidly in some cases, such as that of Çatal Höyük in Anatolia and Mohenjo Daro in the Indian subcontinent (now modern-day Pakistan).

Ancient Architecture

In many ancient civilizations, such as the Egyptians' and Mesopotamians', architecture and urbanism reflected the constant engagement with the divine and the supernatural, and many ancient cultures resorted to monumentality in architecture to represent symbolically the political power of the ruler, the ruling elite, or the state itself.

The architecture and urbanism of the Classical civilizations such as the Greek and the Roman evolved from civic ideals rather than religious or empirical ones and new building types emerged. Architectural styles developed.

Texts on architecture have been written since ancient time. These texts provided both general advice and specific formal prescriptions or canons. Some examples of canons are found in the writings of the 1st-century BCE Roman military engineer Vitruvius, the *Kao Gong Ji* of ancient China and Vaastu Shastra of ancient India and Manjusri Vasthu Vidya Sastra of Sri Lanka. Some of the most important early examples of canonic architecture are religious.

Asian Architecture

The architecture of different parts of Asia developed along different lines from that of Europe; Buddhist, Hindu and Sikh architecture each having different characteristics. Buddhist architecture, in particular, showed great regional diversity. In many Asian countries a pantheistic religion led to architectural forms that were designed specifically to enhance the natural landscape.

Islamic Architecture

Islamic architecture began in the 7th century CE, developing from a blend of architectural forms from the ancient Middle East and from Byzantium but also developing features to suit the religious and social needs of the society. Examples can be found throughout the Middle East, North Africa and Spain, and were to become a significant stylistic influence on European architecture during the Medieval period.

The Medieval Builder

In Europe, in both the Classical and Medieval periods, buildings were not attributed to specific individuals and the names of the architects frequently unknown, despite the vast scale of the many religious buildings extant from this period.

During the Medieval period guilds were formed by craftsmen to organize their trade and written contracts have survived, particularly in relation to ecclesiastical buildings. The role of architect was usually one with that of master mason, or *Magister lathomorum* as they are sometimes described in contemporary documents.

Renaissance and the Architect

With the Renaissance and its emphasis on the individual and humanity rather than religion, and with all its attendant progress and achievements, a new chapter began. Buildings were ascribed to specific architects - Brunelleschi, Alberti, Michelangelo, Palladio - and the cult of the individual had begun.

There was still no dividing line between artist, architect and engineer, or any of the related vocations, and the appellation was often one of regional preference. At this stage, it was still possible for an artist to design a bridge as the level of structural calculations involved was within the scope of the generalist.

Early Modern and the Industrial Age

With the emerging knowledge in scientific fields and the rise of new materials and technology, architecture and engineering began to separate, and the architect began to concentrate on aesthetics and the humanist aspects, often at the expense of technical aspects of building design.

There was also the rise of the "gentleman architect" who usually dealt with wealthy clients and concentrated predominantly on visual qualities derived usually from historical prototypes, typified by the many country houses of Great Britain that were created in the Neo Gothic or

Scottish Baronial styles. Formal architectural training in the 19th century, for example at Ecole des Beaux Arts in France, gave much emphasis to the production of beautiful drawings and little to context and feasibility. Effective architects generally received their training in the offices of other architects, graduating to the role from draughtsmen or clerks.

Meanwhile, the Industrial Revolution laid open the door for mass production and consumption. Aesthetics became a criterion for the middle class as ornamented products, once within the province of expensive craftsmanship, became cheaper under machine production.

Vernacular architecture became increasingly ornamental. House builders could use current architectural design in their work by combining features found in pattern books and architectural journals.

Modernism and Reaction of Architecture

The dissatisfaction with such a general situation at the turn of the twentieth century gave rise to many new lines of thought that served as precursors to Modern Architecture. Notable among these is the Deutscher Werkbund, formed in 1907 to produce better quality machine made objects. The rise of the profession of industrial design is usually placed here. Following this lead, the Bauhaus school, founded in Weimar, Germany in 1919, redefined the architectural bounds prior set throughout history, viewing the creation of a building as the ultimate synthesis—the apex—of art, craft, and technology.

Other architects such as Frank Lloyd Wright developed Organic architecture in which the form was defined by its environment and purpose, with an aim to promote harmony between human habitation and the natural world.

When Modern architecture was first practiced, it was an avant-garde movement with moral, philosophical, and aesthetic underpinnings. Immediately after World War I, pioneering modernist architects sought to develop a completely new style appropriate for a new post-war social and economic order, focused on meeting the needs of the middle and working classes.

They rejected the architectural practice of the academic refinement of historical styles which served the rapidly declining aristocratic order. The approach of the Modernist architects was to reduce buildings to pure forms, removing historical references and ornament in favor of functionalist details. Buildings displayed their functional and structural elements, exposing steel beams and concrete surfaces instead of hiding them behind decorative forms.

Architects such as Mies van der Rohe, Philip Johnson and Marcel Breuer worked to create beauty based on the inherent qualities of building materials and modern construction techniques, trading traditional historic forms for simplified geometric forms, celebrating the new means and methods made possible by the Industrial Revolution, including steel-frame construction, which gave birth to high-rise superstructures. By mid-century, Modernism had morphed into the International Style, an aesthetic epitomized in many ways by the Twin Towers of New York's World Trade Center.

Many architects resisted Modernism, finding it devoid of the decorative richness of ornamented styles. Yet as the founders of that movement lost influence in the late 1970s, Postmodernism developed as a reaction against the austerity of Modernism. Robert Venturi's contention that a "decorated shed" (an ordinary building which is functionally designed inside and embellished on the outside) was better than a "duck" (a building in which the whole form and its function are tied together) gives an idea of this approach.

Architecture Today

Part of the architectural profession, and also some non-architects, responded to Modernism and Postmodernism by going to what they considered the root of the problem. They felt that architecture was not a personal philosophical or aesthetic pursuit by individualists; rather it had to consider everyday needs of people and use technology to give a livable environment.

The *Design Methodology Movement* involving people such as Christopher Alexander started searching for more people-oriented designs. Extensive studies on areas such as behavioral, environmental, and social sciences were done and started informing the design process. As the complexity of buildings began to increase (in terms of structural systems, services, energy and technologies), architecture started becoming more multi-disciplinary. Architecture today usually requires a team of specialist professionals, with the architect being one of many, although usually the team leader.

During the last two decades of the twentieth century and into the new millennium, the field of architecture saw the rise of specializations by project type, technological expertise or project delivery methods. In addition, there has been an increased separation of the 'design' architect from the 'project' architect. Moving the issues of environmental sustainability into the mainstream is a significant development in the architecture profession. Sustainability in architecture was pioneered in the 1960s by architects such as Sim Van der Ryn, in the 1970s Ian McHarg in the US and Brenda and Robert Vale in the UK and New Zealand. There has been an acceleration in the number of buildings which seek to meet green building sustainable design principles.

Sustainable practices that were at the core of vernacular architecture increasingly provide inspiration for environmentally and socially sustainable contemporary techniques. The U.S. Green Building Council's LEED (Leadership in Energy and Environmental Design) rating system has been instrumental in this. An example of an architecturally innovative green building is the Dynamic

Tower which will be powered by wind turbines and solar panels.

Interior Architecture

Interior Architecture is truly a marriage of three distinct design disciplines: interior design, architecture, and industrial design. Interior design focuses on the selection of interior materials, finishes, and furnishings; architecture on the design of building forms and systems; and industrial design on the design of manufactured products.

Another definition is the specific features of a building's interior. It can also be the initial design and plan for use, the later redesign to accommodate a changed purpose, or a significantly revised design for adaptive reuse of the building shell. The latter is often part of sustainable architecture practices, conserving resources through 'recycling' a structure by adaptive redesign. Generally referred to as the spatial art of environmental design, form and practice, interior architecture is the process through which the interiors of buildings are designed, concerned with all aspects of the human uses of structural spaces.

Interior architecture can refer to:

- The art and science of designing and erecting building interiors and related physical features.
- The practice of an interior architect, where architecture means to offer or render professional services in connection with the design and construction of a building's interior that has as its principal purpose human occupancy or use.
- A general term to describe building interiors and related physical features.
- A style or method of design and construction of building interiors and related physical features.

Adaptive Reuse

Although the original spatial hierarchy of a building is always established by its first architect, subsequent iterations of the interior may not be, and for obvious reasons, older structures are often modified by designers of a different generation according to society's changing needs as our cities evolve. This process often re-semanticizes the building as a consequence, and is predicated on the notion that buildings can never really be complete and unalterable.

An altered building may look the same on the exterior, but its interior may be completely different spatially. The interior architect must therefore be sensitive not only to the place of the building in its physical and socio-political context, but to the temporal requirements of changing owners and users. In this sense, if the building has "good bones" the original architectural idea is therefore the first iteration of an internal spatial hierarchy for that structure, after which others are bound to follow

Cities are now dense with such buildings, perhaps originally built as banks that are now restaurants, perhaps industrial mills that are now loft apartments, or even railway stations that have become art galleries. In each case the collective memory of the shape and character of the city is generally held to be more desirable than the possibility of a new building on the same site, although clearly economic forces apply. It is also possible to speculate that there might well be further new interiors for these structures in future years, but for each alteration the technical and technological expertise of the era will determine the extent to which the building is modified in its building life cycle.

Certain structure's interiors remain unaltered over time due to historic preservation, unchanged use, or financial limitations. Nevertheless, most buildings have only three possible long-range internal futures: First, designated significantly important to maintain visually unchanged, only accommodating unseen modern utilities, access, and structural stabilization, and restoration needs. Second, demolished to make way for a new building on the same site, or abandoned, becoming ruins. Finally, redesigned and altered to accommodate new uses.

There are many different degrees of alteration – a minor one to enable the building to conform to new legal codes is likely to prolong the first (or indeed later) iteration of interior space, but a major alteration, such as the retention of only the facade, is to all intents and purposes a new building. All possibilities within and between the two extremes are the domain of the interior architect.

If the practice of Architecture is concerned with the art and science of new building, then the practice of Interior Architecture is concerned with the alteration of existing buildings for new uses.

Earnings

Statistics

Median annual wages of wage-and-salary architects were $70,320 in May 2008. The middle 50 percent earned between $53,480 and $91,870. The lowest 10 percent earned less than $41,320, and the highest 10 percent earned more than $119,220. Those just starting their internships can expect to earn considerably less.

Earnings of partners in established architectural firms may fluctuate because of changing business conditions. Some architects may have difficulty establishing their own practices and may go through a period when their expenses are greater than their income, requiring substantial financial resources.

Many firms pay tuition and fees toward continuing education requirements for their employees.

Education

Purpose

Education in interior architecture should include the study of historic architectural and design styles, building codes and safety, preserving and restoring old buildings, drawing plans of original designs, and building physical and virtual (computer-based) models. The field of interior architecture has a lot in common with interior design and decorating; however, it typically focuses on architecture and construction. Students of both fields learn to design comfortable, safe, and useful indoor spaces, from downtown penthouses to high school classrooms. A student of interior architecture will learn about much more than artistic concerns, such as choosing which style of furnishings works well in an open, loft-like apartment. Study will also include information on technical issues, such as seismic retrofitting (making old buildings safe from earthquakes).

Degree Programs

Interior Architecture stands at the intersection of architecture, design of the built environment, and conservation. Interior architecture programs address the design issues intrinsic to the re-use and transformation of existing structures through both an innovative and progressive approach.

The National Center for Education Statistics states that the definition of a degree program in interior architecture is: "A program that prepares individuals to apply architectural principles in the design of structural interiors for living, recreational, and business purposes and to function as professional interior architects. Study includes instruction in architecture, occupational and safety standards, structural systems design, heating and cooling systems design, interior design, specific end-use applications, and professional responsibilities and standards."

In addition to earning a degree in interior architecture, general licensure is required to work within the United States and some states have further licensing requirements. In many European countries the use of the title "Interior Architect" is legally regulated. This means that a practicing professional cannot use the title of "Interior Architect" unless they complete the requirements for becoming a registered or licensed architect as well as completing a degree program.

General Contractor

A general contractor is responsible for the day-to-day oversight of the construction site, and management of vendors and trades. In addition, keep communication between the general contractor and the involved parties open and clear through out the course of project.

Before starting a job, the general contractor must first visit and then assess the site. As a result of this, the contractor will generate a price, also called an "estimate". The general contractor considers the cost of materials, equipment as well as the cost of labor to provide the owner with an approximate price for the project.

In these contract documents, the contract agreement includes budget, the general and special conditions and the plans and specification of the project that are prepared by a design professional such as an architect. In many instances the general contractor is the project engineer or project manager for construction projects.

Responsibilities

A general contractor is responsible for providing all of the material, labor, equipment, (engineering vehicles and tools) and services necessary for the construction of the project. In order to get these tasks done, the general contractor hires more specialized subcontractors to perform portions or all of the construction work.

Depending on the size of a project, responsibilities may include:

- Filing for building permits,
- Securing the property,
- Providing temporary utilities on site
- Managing personnel on site
- Providing site surveying and engineering
- Disposing/Recycling of construction waste
- Monitoring schedules and cash flows
- Maintaining accurate records as construction progress.

In the United Kingdom and certain former British Commonwealth countries the term 'general contractor' was gradually superseded by 'main contractor' during the early twentieth century. This followed the practice of major professional, trade and consumer organizations issuing standard forms of contract for undertaking the variety of construction works spanning the whole spectrum of the industry. It was and is usual for the term main contractor to be used and defined in all these contract documents, and as a result the term general contractor became an anachronism.

General contractors that conduct work for government agencies are typically referred to as prime contractors.

Requirements for Licensing

There are no set educational requirements to become a general contractor, although most employers do prefer that you have a bachelor's degree. Some general contractors obtain bachelor's degrees in construction science, building science, surveying, construction safety etc.

General contractors usually start out as regular construction workers. While gaining work experience, they learn about different aspects of construction, including masonry, carpentry, framing and plumbing. Aspiring general contractors network with subcontractors and may learn the management skills they need to run their own company.

Depending on the state, the requirements will vary from passing a written exam on topics such as contracting and construction law or require a bachelor's degree for licensing. Utah and Florida are two of the only states that require you having six continuing education credits to maintain a license; this is to protect the general public from fraud, misrepresentation and safety issues. (Included in this requirement are three hours of "core" training and three hours of "professional" training)

Also, all applicants applying for a Utah Contractor's License are required to take the Utah Business and Law exam. The test covers state and federal laws, accounting procedures, construction trade licensing acts, taxes, mechanic lien laws, OSHA requirements, risk management and other general business law questions. To help contractors get ready for this exam, they can visit Utah Division of Occupational and Professional Licensing (DOPL) or Contractor's School, Inc.

Experience in the construction industry as well as references from customers, business partners or former employers are demanded. Some states go as far as requiring candidates to prove financing to own their own general contracting firm. General contractors often run their own business. They hire subcontractors to complete specialized construction work and may manage a team of plumbers, electricians, builders, carpenters and other specialists. General contractors build their business by networking with potential clients, buying basic construction tools and ensuring that their subcontractors complete high-quality work. General contractors don't usually complete much construction work themselves, but they should remain familiar with construction techniques so they can manage workers effectively.

Because general contractors are usually at the top of the employment line the only benefits are the ones that they buy themselves. However, if the general contractor works under a company, getting heath insurance is a plus. Because the jobs vary in complexity, they get paid by the job. Also, some materials cost more than others. For example, tiling a bathroom will cost more than putting siding on a house.

Advantages

One of the biggest advantages is being your own boss, as a contractor you are not required to accept work from a client. You have the freedom to pick and choose your contracts which can result in having a great work variation. Contractors usually take projects that last 3, 6, or 12 months, in duration, to gain a wealth of experience.

Disadvantages

If you own your own business which is common in general contracting, then you must supply yourself and your employees with some health benefits. In addition, taking any paid vacation because you get paid at the end of a job which leads to another problem which is not getting paid. Luckily, if the owner doesn't want to pay you, then filing a contractor's "lien" can help secure payment.

As an Owner

Occasionally the entity commissioning the construction of the building chooses to act as the general contractor. In such cases, they work directly with the subcontractors and take care of the administration and organization of the various subcontractors.

Under these conditions the owner takes on all liability for proper sequencing of the work, and dealing with the realities of construction.

Owners considering this approach, should keep in mind that general contractors make a living working with known subcontractors. An established general contractor will have established relationships that will outlast one construction project, and the subcontractors will acknowledge this with their cooperation. Owners seldom have this advantage, and most subcontractors will recognize the risk of working with a one time client with higher bids.

As an alternative, the owner builder approach to building its own residence can have risks and benefits. As a novice in the business, the owner builder is vulnerable to a number of common mistakes such as overbuilding the neighborhood, exposure to liabilities, lack of subcontractor management skills, and others. Subcontractor loyalty and discounted prices to general contractor are not a rule at all. As the economy worsens, and many builders struggle to find work, the owner builder can pick the best talent at the price that is only limited to his or her negotiating skills.

As a Business Owner

For legal reasons it can be easier to hire and also release a contractor compared to an employee that has Permanent employment. Large numbers of business owners choose to hire contractors because of uncertainty within their business or have constraints such as maternity, illness or other legal factors which entail that hiring a permanent employee is not a feasible option.

General Contractor Example

An owner or real estate developer would develop a program of their needs and select a site (often with an architect). The Architect assembles a design team of consulting engineers and other experts to design the building and specify the building systems to meet those needs. Today contractors frequently participate in the design team effort by providing pre-design services where they will help in providing more accurate estimation of budget and scheduling during design to improve the over all economy of the project.

Otherwise the general contractor is hired just to build the building(s) at the close of the design phase. The owner, architect, and general contractor work closely together to meet deadlines and budget. The general contractor then works with subcontractors to ensure quality standards in addition to timeline and budget. Often there will be disagreements between the contractor and the architect over style vs. function. These arguments may lead to lawsuits which can potentially prolong or even stop a project.

8

THE GROWTH STRATEGIES OF HOTEL INVESTMENT

The Kingdom of Saudi Arabia is placing an increasing focus on developing its tourism market, in a targeted and structured manner, as it seeks to diversify away from oil. There is significant investment being undertaken in tourism infrastructure, including airport expansions and high-speed rail lines, as well as government financed training programmes and public-private partnerships, whilst visa procedures have been eased for non-religious and business visitors.

Furthermore, being home to two of Islam's holiest cities, Al Madinah and Makkah, which attracts millions of Muslims each year for hajj, the world's largest annual pilgrimage, the hotel market is underpinned by Islamic tourism. There is also a high rate of domestic tourism, and the government has put in place initiatives to increase the number of Saudi's that holiday within the Kingdom.

This focus means that, according to a recent report by Business Monitor International, tourist arrivals to the Kingdom are forecast to grow by 5% year on year to 12.91 million in 2010, having remained steady in 2009, at just over 12 million. Year on year, arrivals per annum is expected to average 6.5% growth through to the end of 2014.

A report in March 2009 by the World Travel & Tourism Council, forecast that in 2009 the travel and tourism sector was expected to generate US$27.2 billion (SAE 102.0 billion) of economic activity, equivalent to 7.2% of total Gross Domestic Product, and this is set to rise to 9.2% (SAE 293.4 billion or US$78.4 billion) by 2019. Direct industry employment was expected to rise from 7.3% of total employment in the Kingdom in 2009 to 9.4%, equating to around 922,000 jobs, by 2019.

The potential is illustrated by government plans, announced in February 2010, to build a $13 billion 'tourist city' in Al-Oqair, just south of Al-Khobar on the Kingdom's eastern coast, and on the Red Sea coast, the government has identified sites for development in Tabuk, Yanbu, Makkah, Asir and Jizan provinces. The SCTA has stated that the planned Red Sea resorts would lead to a total of 557,000 hotel rooms being brought online, creating 413,000 jobs in the process.

A number of major international brands are already expanding their presence in Saudi Arabia. The Rezidor Hotel Group has already opened six hotels in the Kingdom, in Jeddah, Riyadh, Yanbu, Al Madinah and Al Khobar, totalling over 1,323 rooms, and has a further four hotels, with over 1,000 combined rooms, under development, across three different locations.

Kurt Ritter, President and CEO of The Rezidor Hotel Group, commented: "Saudi Arabia is a hugely important market for us, and in 2009 we were delighted to open a further two developments in the country. The key aspect for us is the diversity of the market, allowing us to introduce different brands into the Kingdom, which include Radisson Blu and Park Inn at the moment, with a particular focus on serving religious and cultural visitors. I have no doubt that the opportunities will keep growing, which is why we have a number of additional hotels in the pipeline."

One of the world's largest hotel companies, Wyndham Hotel Group, is also expanding its presence in the region. In November 2009, the Hotel Group signed an agreement for the first Wyndham branded hotel in the Middle East, the Wyndham Riyadh located in Saudi Arabia. That property will join the company's growing portfolio of 28 hotels already operational in the Middle East, including Ramada Worldwide's largest hotel, the 998-room hotel in the holy city of Makkah.

Eric Danziger, President and CEO of Wyndham Hotel Group, commented: "The Middle East plays a significant role in Wyndham Hotel Group's global growth strategy. We are so pleased to already have a significant presence in the Kingdom of Saudi Arabia and numerous properties throughout the region. We have focused our efforts in the market and in the last year we announced some of our newest developments including the 299-room Ramada®Plaza Kuwait hotel and the 183-room Ramada Hotel and Suites Amman hotel. We also celebrated the signing of an agreement for the Ramada Encore Doha hotel, a first in the Middle East for the brand".

Kurt Ritter and Eric Danziger will be speaking on the 'Leaders' Panel – Global and MENA Hotel Investment Opportunities' at AHIC 2010.

Jonathan Worsley, Chairman of Bench Events which co-organises AHIC, commented: "The hotel investment market in Saudi Arabia is extremely exciting, with a need for quality product, ranging from high-end luxury resorts to mid-market and budget hotel developments. The government is working hard to put in place measured tourism expansion plans, but it is important that investors understand what opportunities are there and how they are accessed, and our line-up of speakers will be able to offer significant insight on that front."

The Saudi Commission for Tourism and Antiquities (SCTA), the national authority responsible for the planning and development of domestic tourism, is also leading government efforts to promote more inbound travel, and will be represented at AHIC by Dr Salah K AlBukkayet, Vice President – Investment.

"Condotels," also known as "condo hotels," are typically condominiums in resort or downtown communities. A condotel looks and feels to visitors like a hotel or resort, but in these resorts, individuals have the opportunity to purchase individual units.

Unlike a timeshare, where buyers pay for limited use of a resort, buyers of a condotel own their residence outright and can stay in it, rent it out, or sell it according to their own wishes.

In these communities, in-house management companies rent out the units on behalf of their owners in exchange for a percentage of the rental income. Condotel owners and their renters often have use of the resort's amenities, such as concierge, fitness and spa services.

Whether an owner can use the amenities while a renting guest is staying in the unit depends on the rules of the particular condotel development. These condos make up a relatively new investment category and account for less than 10% of all vacation homes and investment properties in the U.S., according to the National Association of Realtors.

Owning a condotel differs from buying and managing a condo in several respects, says Joel Greene, president of Condo Hotel Center in Miami, a real-estate agency that specializes in the sale of condo hotels throughout the country.

Unlike typical condos built by multifamily housing developers, condotels are often developed by hotel and resort companies — such as Starwood Hotels & Resorts Worldwide, Hilton Hotels Corp., The Ritz-Carlton Hotel Company, LLC, and Four Seasons Hotels and Resorts. The price you pay for a unit may be substantially higher than that for a "regular" condo.

For the extra cost, you have access to the services of an in-house management company, which will market and rent your unit out for long or short periods of time (even nightly).

The management company's rental program will charge you a portion of your rental income (typically 50%), and will handle the maintenance of your unit, grounds keeping and the clean-up after your renters leave. It will also oversee guest amenities such as pools, tennis courts and golf courses.

If you bought a "regular" condo and hired an outside management firm to market and lease your unit to renters, there may be less flexibility when it comes to placing your unit in and out of the rental program, and the firm may not market your unit nationally in the way that a large hotel company might, Mr. Greene says.

When looking to invest in a condotel, research the local real-estate market (e.g., are prices on the rise, or has the real-estate market peaked?). Study regional tourist activity and hotel occupancy, since a condotel unit, especially if it is run by a hotel operator, may be marketed like a hotel room.

The location of your unit has the potential of figuring prominently into how profitable an investment it is.

Jerry Yeiter, past president of The National Real Estate Investors Association and president of Yeiter & Co., an accounting firm in Houston, says some investors have had success with condotels in Florida and Arizona because these destinations offer desirable tourist activities and because these buyers purchased at a time when area real-estate prices were appreciating.

Ask yourself whether Branson can attract tourists. I checked with the Branson Lakes Area Chamber of Commerce and Convention and Visitors Bureau, and was told by Jennifer McCullough, public relations director, that Branson, which is in the Ozark Mountains, draws more than seven million tourists a year.

Factoring in visitors who stay in rented vacation condos, the combined hotel and condo occupancy rate in Branson is 62% to 63%, according to the town's chamber of commerce and convention and visitors bureau.

If you buy before a condotel project is fully built, you may be able to purchase your unit at a lower cost, as developers tend to offer the lowest prices pre-construction. You may have to wait until the project is completed, though, before you can rent out your unit. Estimate how much you can fetch per night and how often you need to rent the unit out to bring in enough to cover your mortgage and other expenses.

"It's all about the numbers," Mr. Yeiter says. "You'd have to look at the rules and make sure the property would be suitable for an investor." Some management companies, for example, stipulate how often you must make your place available and even how it should be decorated.

Investment management is the professional management of various securities (shares, bonds and other securities) and assets (e.g., real estate) in order to meet specified investment goals for the benefit of the investors. Investors may be institutions (insurance companies, pension funds, corporations etc.) or private investors (both directly via investment contracts and more commonly via collective investment schemes e.g. mutual funds or exchange-traded funds).

The term asset management is often used to refer to the investment management of collective investments, (not necessarily) while the more generic fund management may refer to all forms of institutional investment as well as investment management for private investors. Investment managers who specialize in *advisory* or *discretionary* management on behalf of (normally wealthy) private investors may often refer to their services as wealth management or portfolio management often within the context of so-called "private banking".

The provision of 'investment management services' includes elements of financial statement analysis, asset selection, stock selection, plan implementation and ongoing monitoring of investments. Investment management is a large and important global industry in its own right responsible for caretaking of trillions of yuan, dollars, euro, pounds and yen. Coming under the remit of financial services many of the world's largest companies are at least in part investment managers and employ millions of staff and create billions in revenue.

Fund manager (or investment adviser in the United States) refers to both a firm that provides investment management services and an individual who directs fund management decisions.

It has several facets, including the employment of professional fund managers, research (of individual assets and asset classes), dealing, settlementis difficult to sustain, and clients may not be patient during times of poor performance;

· successfstitution polls, should it then: (i) Vote the entire holding as directed by the majority of votes cast? (ii) Split the vote (where this is allowed) according to the proportions of the vote? (iii) Or respect the abstainers and only vote the respondents' holdings?

The price signals generated by large active managers holding or not holding the stock may contribute to management change. For example, this is the case when a large active manager sells his position in a company, leading to (possibly) a decline in the stock price, but more importantly a loss of confidence by the markets in the management of the company, thus precipitating changes in the management team.

Some institutions have been more vocal and active in pursuing such matters; for instance, some firms believe that there are investment advantages to accumulating substantial minority shareholdings (i.e. 10% or more) and putting pressure on management to implement significant changes in the business. In some cases, institutions with minority holdings work together to force management change. Perhaps more frequent is the sustained pressure that large institutions bring to bear on management teams through persuasive discourse and PR.

On the other hand, some of the largest investment managers—such as BlackRock and Vanguard—advocate simply owning every company, reducing the incentive to influence management teams. A reason for this last strategy is that the investment manager prefers a closer, more open and honest relationship with a company's management team than would exist if they exercised control; allowing them to make a better investment decision.

The national context in which shareholder representation considerations are set is variable and important. The USA is a litigious society and shareholders use the law as a lever to pressure management teams. In Japan it is traditional for shareholders to be low in the 'pecking order,' which often allows management and labor to ignore the rights of the ultimate owners. Whereas US firms generally cater to shareholders, Japanese businesses generally exhibit a *stakeholder* mentality, in which they seek consensus amongst all interested parties (against a background of strong unions and labour legislation).

Size of the Global Fund Management Industry

Conventional assets under management of the global fund management industry increased by 14% in 2009, to $71.3 trillion. Pension assets accounted for $28.0 trillion of the total, with $22.9 trillion invested in mutual funds and $20.4 trillion in insurance funds. Together with alternative assets (sovereign wealth funds, hedge funds, private equity funds and exchange traded funds) and funds of wealthy individuals, assets of the global fund management industry totalled over $105 trillion, an increase of 15% on the previous year.

The increase in 2009 followed a 18% decline in the previous year and was largely a result of the recovery in equity markets during the year. Part of the reason for the increase in dollar terms was the depreciation in the value of the US dollar against a number of currencies in 2009.

The US remained by far the biggest source of funds, accounting for around a half of conventional assets under management or some $36 trillion. The UK was the second largest centre in the world and by far the largest in Europe with around 9% of the global total.

Philosophy, Process and People

The 3-P's (Philosophy, Process and People) are often used to describe the reasons why the manager is able to produce above average results.

- **Philosophy** refers to the over-arching beliefs of the investment organization. For example: (i) Does the manager buy growth or value shares (and why)? (ii) Do they believe in market timing (and on what evidence)? (iii) Do they rely on external research or do they employ a team of researchers? It is helpful if any and all of such fundamental beliefs are supported by proof-statements.
- **Process** refers to the way in which the overall philosophy is implemented. For example: (i) Which universe of assets is explored before particular assets are chosen as suitable investments? (ii) How does the manager decide what to buy and when? (iii) How does the manager decide what to sell and when? (iv) Who takes the decisions and are they taken by committee? (v) What controls are in place to ensure that a rogue

fund (one very different from others and from what is intended) cannot arise?

- **People** refers to the staff, especially the fund managers. The questions are, Who are they? How are they selected? How old are they? Who reports to whom? How deep is the team (and do all the members understand the philosophy and process they are supposed to be using)? And most important of all, How long has the team been working together? This last question is vital because whatever performance record was presented at the outset of the relationship with the client may or may not relate to (have been produced by) a team that is still in place. If the team has changed greatly (high staff turnover or changes to the team), then arguably the performance record is completely unrelated to the existing team (of fund managers).

Investment Managers and Portfolio Structures

At the heart of the investment management industry are the managers who invest and divest client investments.

A certified company investment advisor should conduct an assessment of each client's individual needs and risk profile. The advisor then recommends appropriate investments.

Asset Allocation

The different asset class definitions are widely debated, but four common divisions are stocks, bonds, real-estate and commodities. The exercise of allocating funds among these assets (and among individual securities within each asset class) is what investment management firms are paid for. Asset classes exhibit different market dynamics, and different interaction effects; thus, the allocation of money among asset classes will have a significant effect on the performance of the fund.

Some research suggests that allocation among asset classes has more predictive power than the choice of individual holdings in determining portfolio return. Arguably, the skill of a successful investment manager resides in constructing the asset allocation, and separately the individual holdings, so as to outperform certain benchmarks (e.g., the peer group of competing funds, bond and stock indices).

Long-term Returns

It is important to look at the evidence on the long-term returns to different assets, and to holding period returns (the returns that accrue on average over different lengths of investment). For example, over very long holding periods (e.g. 10+ years) in most countries, equities have generated higher returns than bonds, and bonds have generated higher returns than cash. According to financial theory, this is because equities are riskier (more volatile) than bonds which are themselves more risky than cash.

Diversification

Against the background of the asset allocation, fund managers consider the degree of diversification that makes sense for a given client (given its risk preferences) and construct a list of planned holdings accordingly. The list will indicate what percentage of the fund should be invested in each particular stock or bond. The theory of portfolio diversification was originated by Markowitz (and many others) and effective diversification requires management of the correlation between the asset returns and the liability returns, issues internal to the portfolio (individual holdings volatility), and cross-correlations between the returns.

Investment Styles

There are a range of different styles of fund management that the institution can implement. For example, growth, value, market neutral, small capitalisation, indexed, etc. Each of these approaches has its distinctive features, adherents and, in any particular financial environment, distinctive risk characteristics. For example, there is evidence that growth styles (buying rapidly growing earnings) are especially effective when the companies able to generate such growth are scarce; conversely, when such growth is plentiful, then there is evidence that value styles tend to outperform the indices particularly successfully.

Performance Measurement

Fund performance is often thought to be the acid test of fund management, and in the institutional context, accurate measurement is a necessity. For that purpose, institutions measure the performance of each fund (and usually for internal purposes components of each fund) under their management, and performance is also measured by external firms that specialize in performance measurement. The leading performance measurement firms (e.g. Frank Russell in the USA or BI-SAM in Europe) compile aggregate industry data, e.g., showing how funds in general performed against given indices and peer groups over various time periods.

In a typical case (let us say an equity fund), then the calculation would be made (as far as the client is concerned) every quarter and would show a percentage change compared with the prior quarter (e.g., +4.6% total return in US dollars). This figure would be compared with other similar funds managed within the institution (for purposes of monitoring internal controls), with performance data for peer group funds, and with relevant indices (where available) or tailor-made performance benchmarks where appropriate. The specialist performance measurement firms calculate quartile and decile data and close attention would be paid to the (percentile) ranking of any fund.

Generally speaking, it is probably appropriate for an investment firm to persuade its clients to assess performance over longer periods (e.g., 3 to 5 years) to smooth out very short term fluctuations in performance and the influence of the business cycle. This can be difficult however and, industry wide, there is a serious preoccupation with short-term numbers and the effect on the relationship with clients (and resultant business risks for the institutions).

An enduring problem is whether to measure before-tax or after-tax performance. After-tax measurement represents the benefit to the investor, but investors' tax positions may vary. Before-tax measurement can be misleading, especially in regimens that tax realised capital gains (and not unrealised). It is thus possible that successful active managers (measured before tax) may produce miserable after-tax results. One possible solution is to report the after-tax position of some standard taxpayer.

Risk-adjusted Performance Measurement

Performance measurement should not be reduced to the evaluation of fund returns alone, but must also integrate other fund elements that would be of interest to investors, such as the measure of risk taken. Several other aspects are also part of performance measurement: evaluating if managers have succeeded in reaching their objective, i.e. if their return was sufficiently high to reward the risks taken; how they compare to their peers; and finally whether the portfolio management results were due to luck or the manager's skill.

The need to answer all these questions has led to the development of more sophisticated performance measures, many of which originate in modern portfolio theory. Modern portfolio theory established the quantitative link that exists between portfolio risk and return.

The Capital Asset Pricing Model (CAPM) developed by Sharpe (1964) highlighted the notion of rewarding risk and produced the first performance indicators, be they risk-adjusted ratios (Sharpe ratio, information ratio) or differential returns compared to benchmarks (alphas). The Sharpe ratio is the simplest and best known performance measure. It measures the return of a portfolio in excess of the risk-free rate, compared to the total risk of the portfolio. This measure is said to be absolute, as it does not refer to any benchmark, avoiding drawbacks related to a poor choice of benchmark.

Meanwhile, it does not allow the separation of the performance of the market in which the portfolio is invested from that of the manager. The information ratio is a more general form of the Sharpe ratio in which the risk-free asset is replaced by a benchmark portfolio. This measure is relative, as it evaluates portfolio performance in reference to a benchmark, making the result strongly dependent on this benchmark choice.

Portfolio alpha is obtained by measuring the difference between the return of the portfolio and that of a benchmark portfolio. This measure appears to be the only reliable performance measure to evaluate active management. In fact, we have to distinguish between normal returns, provided by the fair reward for portfolio exposure to different risks, and obtained through passive management, from abnormal performance (or outperformance) due to the manager's skill (or luck), whether through market timing, stock picking, or good fortune.

The first component is related to allocation and style investment choices, which may not be under the sole control of the manager, and depends on the economic context, while the second component is an evaluation of the success of the manager's decisions. Only the latter, measured by alpha, allows the evaluation of the manager's true performance (but then, only if you assume that any outperformance is due to skill and not luck).

Portfolio return may be evaluated using factor models. The first model, proposed by Jensen (1968), relies on the CAPM and explains portfolio returns with the market index as the only factor. It quickly becomes clear, however, that one factor is not enough to explain the returns very well and that other factors have to be considered. Multi-factor models were developed as an alternative to the CAPM, allowing a better description of portfolio risks and a more accurate evaluation of a portfolio's performance. For example, Fama and French (1993) have highlighted two important factors that characterize a company's risk in addition to market risk. These factors are the book-to-market ratio and the company's size as measured by its market capitalization.

Fama and French therefore proposed three-factor model to describe portfolio normal returns (Fama-French three-factor model). Carhart (1997) proposed to add momentum as a fourth factor to allow the short-term persistence of returns to be taken into account. Also of interest for performance measurement is Sharpe's (1992) style analysis model, in which factors are style indices. This model allows a custom benchmark for each portfolio to be developed, using the linear combination of style indices that best replicate portfolio style allocation, and leads to an accurate evaluation of portfolio alpha

Education or Certification

Increasingly, international business schools are incorporating the subject into their course outlines and some have formulated the title of 'Investment Management' or 'Asset Management' conferred as specialist bachelor's degrees (e.g. Cass Business School, London). Due to global cross-recognition agreements with the 2 major accrediting agencies AACSB and ACBSP which accredit over 560 of the best business school programs, the Certification of MFP Master Financial Planner Professional from the American Academy of Financial Management is available to AACSB and ACBSP business school graduates with finance or financial services-related concentrations.

For people with aspirations to become an investment manager, further education may be needed beyond a bachelors in business, finance, or economics. Designations, such as the CIM in Canada, are required for practitioners in the investment management industry. A graduate degree or an investment qualification such as the Chartered Financial Analyst designation (CFA) or the Certified Financial Markets Practitioner (CFMP) Exam by the Management Laboratory may help in having a career in investment management.

There is no evidence that any particular qualification enhances the most desirable characteristic of an investment manager, that is the ability to select investments that result in an above average (risk weighted) long-term performance. The industry has a tradition of seeking out, employing and generously rewarding such people without reference to any formal qualifications.

Miramar Hotel and Investment

Miramar Hotel and Investment Company Limited is a hotel chain company in Hong Kong. Its core businesses include property rental and development, hotel operation and management, travel services and food & beverage services. The group now manages a total of nine hotels in Hong Kong and Mainland China including The Mira Hotel.

The group was founded in 1957 by Mr. Young Chi Wan after taking over the Spanish Catholic Missions-owned hotel property on Nathan Road, Kowloon. It was listed on the Hong Kong Stock Exchange in 1970. It was also a member of

Hang Seng Index Constituent Stocks (blue-chip stocks) from 1974 to 1996. In 1993, it was acquired by Henderson Investment, a subsidiary of Henderson Land Development.

Legacy Hotels Real Estate Investment Trust

Legacy Hotels Real Estate Investment Trust was a real estate investment trust (REIT) that was based in Toronto, Ontario. It was established in 1997 and was owner of 24 hotel and resort properties most of which are located in Canada, but it also had a couple in the United States. Its hotels operate under the Fairmont and Delta names.

It had a 24% stake in Fairmont, the rest held by Colony Capital and Kingdom Holding Company. The company was acquired by LGY Acquisition LP effective September 18, 2007, and delisted from the Toronto Stock Exchange.

Kingdom Holding Company

Kingdom Holding Company is a public holding company headquartered in Kingdom Centre in Riyadh, Saudi Arabia, and is the largest company in Saudi Arabia. It is controlled by Prince Alwaleed Bin Talal Bin Abdulaziz, and is headquartered in the city of Riyadh. The company is publicly listed in the Saudi Stock Exchange but only 6% of the shares are public, the rest is privately owned with the majority stakeholder, Prince Alwaleed holding 94% shares.

The company describes itself as a diversified investment company, whose interests include banking, real estate, telecommunications, broadcasting and media, entertainment, hospitality, computers and electronics, agriculture, restaurants, upscale fashion, retailing, supermarkets, tourism, travel and automotive manufacturing.

Its international investments include (or have included)

- Amazon
- AOL/Time Warner

- Apple Inc.
- Canary Wharf
- Citigroup
- Coca Cola
- Compaq
- Disneyland Paris
- Four Seasons Hotels & Resorts
- Fairmont Hotels & Resorts
- Ford
- Hotel George V, Paris
- Hewlett-Packard
- McDonald's
- Motorola
- Mövenpick Hotels & Resorts
- News Corporation
- PepsiCo
- Priceline.com Inc
- The Walt Disney Company
- LBCI Lebanese Broadcasting Corporation International
- SAMBA, Saudi American Bank
- Rotana Group the Arab World's largest entertainment company
- Kingdom Hotels International, public company listed on the Dubai International Financial Exchange

The company is known for hiring in 2004 Captain Hanadi Zakariya Hindi, the first Saudi female commercial pilot, who trained at the Mideast Aviation Academy in Jordan.

It is also the owner of the Kingdom Centre. In July 2005, Kingdom announced a joint venture with HSBC to invest in growth companies in Sub-Saharan Africa. The company committed to purchasing 1 A380 aircraft from Airbus for an undisclosed amount.

Pan Pacific Hotels Growth Plan

Pan Pacific Hotels Group shares strategy for growth at the Hospitality Investment Conference Asia Pacific in Hong Kong. Pan Pacific Hotels Group revealed at the Hospitality Investment Conference Asia Pacific (HICAP) the strategic moves it has made to prime itself and its two brands Pan Pacific and PARKROYAL for growth.

At the three-day HICAP event in Hong Kong, attended by close to 700 investors, financiers, developers and leading industry professionals from around the world, the Group also spoke about how its business model and brands can offer hotel owners a viable and profitable alternative to big hotel chains.

Human-Scale Operations and Solutions

Speaking at the 'Small is Beautiful – Operator/ Branding Alternatives to the Big Chains' session, Pan Pacific Hotels Group Senior Vice President of Development, Eric Levy highlighted how the Group's modest size translates into flexibility and agility in offering solutions to individual properties and its owners.

"Our size and consequent shortened lines of communications has great significance to how we interact and work with our hotel owners; it's not about whether you can speak to the CEO, but when you can speak with the CEO," said Eric Levy. "We are able to offer focused and customised solutions for each property and issue, instead of offering formulas and templates."

Looking Inward to Grow Outwards

The Group's Vice President of Operations Dennis Wright, who spoke at the workshop 'How to Manage Asset Profitability by Maximizing Revenue during Volatile Times' stressed the need for hotel operators to relook their hotel property and competitor set as a guest, instead of a hotelier.

"By identifying key guest expectations and then taking the necessary steps to exceed them in quantifiable areas, you will effectively gain customer loyalty to your brand," said Dennis Wright. "Step out of the box and look inside; in times like these, building strong brands requires us to exceed customer expectations, not compromise them."

Turning Tough Times into Opportunity

This year marks an important chapter of Pan Pacific Hotels Group's growth. Integrating both the Pan Pacific and PARKROYAL brands under it in April this year, the Group has also invested in its brands with the appointment of global brand strategists Interbrand to conduct a brand review on both Pan Pacific and PARKROYAL brands. Now recently concluded, the review aims to refresh the value propositions of the two brands to prime them for future growth.

In August this year, Pan Pacific Hotels Group opened Pan Pacific Xiamen while Pan Pacific Suzhou will open on 11 January 2010. A brand new hotel in Tianjin is also scheduled for completion in 2012. In addition, Pan Pacific Serviced Suites Bangkok is due to launch in January 2010, and that will follow with the opening of PARKROYAL Serviced Suites Kuala Lumpur in May 2010.

These moves mark Pan Pacific Hotels Group's efforts in realising its growth strategy, focused on expanding its hotel portfolio aggressively in the key markets of China, Southeast Asia, North America and Australia.

Hotel Investment Leaders Like the Future

Like most other speakers and attendees at Americas Lodging Investment Summit, the big dogs of hotel financing were enthusiastic about the next couple of years. The final session at ALIS brought together eight members of IREFAC, the industry's top investment and financing think tank, and their consensus was for a bright future for lenders, borrowers and owners.

"We're right to be bullish," said Four Seasons Hotels President and CEO Kathleen Taylor. "We have huge momentum, both domestically and globally, both through the sheer growth in our existing business and the additional opportunities we see for new development or conversions in emerging markets."

The panelists were in awe of the speed of the recovery, a trend that has been recognized by investors in REIT and hotel company C-corp stocks, the share prices of which have risen between 30 and 40 percent in the past year.

"These investors may be a little ahead of the curve, but they see the future correctly," said Mike Shannon, managing director of KSL Capital Partners. "In an era in which the alternatives are low-yield investments, public equity, including hotel stocks, looks pretty good right now."

While public companies have been very active in hotel acquisitions, a thawing of the debt markets should make it more viable for private companies looking to make transactions. One panelist, Gary Mendell, chairman and CEO of HEI Hotels & Resorts, a private firm, employs a strategy that veers from the focus of most public companies.

"Since they're mostly looking at center cities in the top 10 major markets, we're sellers of assets in those markets and are moving into secondary, but still major markets—cities like Atlanta and others in California and Florida—where the REITs are less focused at this time," said Mendell.

Bidding against a public company can be daunting, he said, citing a recent deal in which HEI bid $102 million for an asset that a public company ultimately bid and won for about $120 million.

The panel generally agreed lenders are becoming less likely to extend or modify loans for hotel assets that may be in distress, although as Michael Murphy, head of hospitality and leisure capital at First Fidelity, said a loan backed by a good sponsor with a strong relationship to the lender has a better chance of extension. "And as it turns out, banks have been rewarded by the slowness in acting as valuations on assets are creeping back up."

Mendell had an even simpler formula to explain lender behavior: "We've been successful in extending debt if the asset is worth less than the debt on it. However, if the asset is worth more than the debt, it's more likely the lender wants us to sell."

Jackson Hsieh, vice chairman of UBS, believes (as did many other ALIS speakers) the CMBS market for hotel financing will roar back in 2011. He said his firm issued no CMBS loans in 2009 but did about $1.2 billion in the past year, nearly all in the past 60 days. "We expect Wall Street will do about $30 billion this year. What the market really needs, however, is floating-rate CMBS, which I think will develop later in the year," said Hsieh.

Despite the upturn in hotel performance and a loosening of the lending markets, financing for new construction is not yet widely available, said the panel. "If you're a lender and you can make conservative loans on existing product as values are coming off the bottom, why would you take a risk on new construction?" asked Mark Elliott, senior managing director of Hodges Ward Elliott.

Murphy offered up a telling example of the problems in obtaining financing for new hotel construction. His firm worked with a potential borrower with high net worth and willing to take a non-recourse loan for a project that had a top brand, in a good market with excellent management.

"We were confident we could get it done, but we went to more than 70 sources of capital over an extended period of time and flogged the deal in every way possible," he said. "The reaction of most lenders to a hospitality construction deal like this was as though we reached in our pocket and put a rat on the table."

Like all prudent business people, the panelists see potential risks on the horizon for the industry and the financing environment. Four Seasons' Taylor echoed several panelists with her concern over global issues, particularly continued economic uncertainties. "Any upset in the world—economies, terrorism, drug wars, whatever—affects our industry," she said. "On the positive side, a recovery in global economies will provide strong tailwinds for brands like mine that are trying to expand internationally."

KSL's Shannon is more concerned about possible rises in interest rates and inflation. "Inflation will be back, and employees who didn't get raises in the last couple of years will see our revenues increasing and they'll want a piece of it," said Shannon. "The challenge will be controlling these and all other costs."

Despite the concerns, the panelists are still extremely bullish on the long-term investment outlook for the hospitality sector of commercial real estate because of the industry's unique attributes.

"Travel and tourism is a very resilient business and it continues to grow in consumer share of wallet," said Shannon. "And private equity is a great model in this industry for those patient investors who are willing to look out 10 to 15 years and are willing to bet on that fundamental resiliency of travel and leisure."

9

THE GROWTH STRATEGIES OF LODGING INDUSTRY

Lodging or a holiday accommodation is a type of residential accommodation. People who travel and stay away from home for more than a day need lodging for sleep, rest, safety, shelter from cold temperatures or rain, storage of luggage and access to common household functions.

Lodgings may be self catering in which case no food is laid on but cooking facilities are available. Lodging is done in a hotel, hostel or hostal, a private home (commercial, i.e. a bed and breakfast, a guest house, a vacation rental, or non-commercially, with members of hospitality services or in the home of friends), in a tent, caravan/camper (often on a campsite). In addition there are make-shift solutions.

Sleeping is typically done lying in a bed, or more generally on a soft surface, such as an air mattress, a couch, etc. Some trains have sleeping cars. Sometimes people sleep sitting, because lying is not possible, such as in a train (if not in a sleeping car), a bus, a seat in a waiting room or a bench on the street or in a park.

Inclinable seats allow something between sitting and lying. Whether lying on a row of seats is possible and comfortable depends on the presence of arm rests, and whether they can be moved up. In some public places, lying would be possible, but is not permitted.

A guest house is a kind of lodging. In some parts of the world a guest house is similar to a hostel, bed and breakfast, or inn whereas in other parts of the world (such as for example the Caribbean), guest houses are a type of inexpensive hotel-like lodging. In still others, it is a private home which has been converted for the exclusive use of guest accommodation. The owner usually lives in an entirely separate area within the property and the guest house may serve as a form of lodging business.

In some areas of the world, guest houses are the only kind of accommodation available for visitors who have no local relatives to stay with. Among the features which distinguish a guest house from a hotel, bed and breakfast, or inn is the lack of a full-time staff.

Guest houses tend to be owner managed, due to their size, although in some countries, such as South Africa, guest houses can be very large mansions indeed. South Africa also has a specific rating system for accommodation establishments.

Bed and breakfasts are usually family-owned, with the family living on the premises. Hotels maintain a staff presence 24 hours a day and 7 days a week, whereas a guest house has a more limited staff presence. Because of limited staff presence, check in at a guest house is often by appointment. An Inn also usually has a restaurant attached.

In Japan, tenants in a guest house have to pay a substantial damage deposit, and have to pay a cleaning fee when they leave.

The hotels and motels we know today evolved from small, one-room, private dwellings that served merchants as early as 500 B.C. From this modest beginning, the hotel industry has come to play a vital role in the development of trade, commerce, and travel throughout the world.

The first record of innkeeping law is found in the Code of Hammurabi, who ruled Babylonia in approximately 2000 B.C. The code sets forth specific regulations for the operation of Babylonian taverns and inns, including corporal penalties for watering down beer. In this period, taverns and inns were prevalent throughout Greece, Italy, Egypt, and Asia. Greek taverns were frequently located near a temple for easy preparation and transportation of sacrificial animals. These establishments provided travelers with food, drink, and sometimes a bed. The Olympic Games, which began in Greece in 776 B.C., involved travel for both spectators and players, creating a demand for accommodations.

During the rise and fall of the Roman Empire, pleasure travel became possible due to good roads, stable government, economic prosperity, and increased leisure time. Educated, affluent Romans vacationed in Greece and toured Egypt. An excellent network of consular roads and post houses was developed to handle this increased travel demand.

After the fall of the Roman Empire in A.D. 476, travel and trade dropped significantly. The Middle Ages was a time of unstable politics and danger on the roads. Religious travelers were common, however, as the church increased its dominance. Religious orders provided accommodations for travelers in monasteries and in the hospices and inns they operated. Most trips during this period were pilgrimages to holy sites or journeys to fight in the Crusades, which began in A.D. 1095 and lasted approximately 200 years.

In the 13th century the innkeepers of Florence, Italy, formed the first hotel guild. Guild members interviewed visitors at the city gate, assigning foreigners to certain lodging facilities and local visitors to others. Most guild members did not own their hostelries; they rented them under three-year leases from the city.

A resurgence in lodging demand started in England during the Industrial Revolution (1760), when the British government arranged for mail to be delivered by coach. A national posting system was created and a network of posting inns was established to accommodate the young postboys and provide a change of horses. Travel by coach became fashionable and long coach trips gave rise to demand for overnight lodging and the development of the English inn. These lodging facilities, forerunners of the modern motel, were located on coach trails to provide refuge for weary travelers and protection from highwaymen. Accommodations in these inns typically consisted of single, unheated rooms with straw beds for the nobility and common sleeping areas on stone floors for their servants. Travelers and local townspeople alike enjoyed hearty food and drink.

The American counterpart of the English inn was the colonial inn and tavern. Such inns sprang up in seaport towns and along stagecoach roads and canals in the 1700s and 1800s. In addition to providing travelers with overnight accommodations, colonial inns were often public gathering places used for courts of law, town meetings, and school classes. Massachusetts recognized the importance of inns to statewide commerce and passed a law penalizing any town that did not provide this convenience.

The following description of a colonial inn illustrates how far American hostelries have come in 200 years:

Accommodations often meant sleeping on the floor of the "long room," with one's feet turned toward the fireplace and one's head on a rolled-up coat, alongside a dozen or more other persons of both sexes. It meant a quick cold-water wash in an outdoor basin and gingerly use of a communal towel. A warning blast on the landlord's cow horn meant all hands to table, ready to tackle breakfast with fingers and knives.

Over time the accommodations provided by colonial inns gradually improved in response to the needs of a mobile, restless society, and American innkeepers assumed their place as important community figures. Samuels Coles of Boston, who opened one of the first taverns in America, became a leading church member and a steward of Harvard University. Because inns functioned as centers of political and social activity, their owners and operators were community leaders.

The First Hotels

The first hotel constructed in the United States was the 73-room City Hotel located at 115 Broadway in downtown New York City. Completed in 1794, the City Hotel was enormous compared to colonial inns and served as a model for similar establishments in Boston, Philadelphia, and Baltimore.

Boston's first hotel was the Exchange Coffee House (1806), which boasted seven stories and 200 rooms, many overlooking a five-story, domed interior courtyard (a forerunner of the atrium hotel). Philadelphia's first hotel, the Mansion House, was built in 1807. Baltimore followed, opening the Baltimore City Hotel in 1826. Each of these properties was larger and more lavish than its predecessor and became the focus of civic pride.

During the 1800s hotels moved westward and flourished in major American cities and towns. The Tremont House in Boston started a trend toward luxury accommodations by offering unheard-of services and amenities: private guestrooms, doors with locks, a washbowl with a water pitcher and free soap, bellboys, French cuisine, and an annunciator system that allowed the front desk to contact guests in their rooms.

Spurred by the success of the Tremont House, hotels nationwide attempted to outdo each other in size, luxury and inventiveness. In 1836 the Astor House in New York City installed steam-powered pumps to send water up above the first-floor level so that plumbing could be installed on upper floors. The New York Hotel, built in 1844, was the first hotel to provide private baths connected to some of its bedrooms, while the Buffalo Statler, built in 1908, included private baths in all of its guestrooms. In 1835 the American Hotel in New York City was the first to have gaslight throughout the building. Edison's electric light was first installed in the public areas of the Hotel Everett in 1882, and the Sagamore Hotel, which opened in 1883 on Lake George, New York, was the first to have electric lights throughout. In 1894 the Hotel Netherlands in New York City installed the first hotel telephone system. The Fifth Avenue Hotel in New York City was the first to have elevators, an innovation that later enabled hotels to be constructed as high-rise structures. The first fully air-conditioned hotel was the Detroit Statler.

As the number of hotels increased, many properties faced the prospect of rapid obsolescence and a consequent loss in value. The City Hotel, for example, became obsolete within 15 years due to competition and was converted into an office building 38 years later. The trend-setting Tremont House closed for major modernization after 20 years of operation and was considered a second-class property during the last two decades of its 65-year life. Today hostelries face similar problems due to constant changes in modes of transportation and customer preferences as well as competition from newer properties.

The hotels of the mid-1800s followed the railroads westward, and ornate, luxury properties were constructed at major rail centers: the Palmer House in Chicago (1882), Brown Palace in Denver (1893), and the Palace in San Francisco (1875). Hotels became status symbols, and cities tried to outdo each other by building larger and more expensive facilities. In many cases the hotels developed far exceeded existing or potential markets.

In addition to luxurious city hotels, resort hotels were introduced as new rail lines enabled affluent Americans to travel on vacation. Spas, which were considered the first American resorts, were opened in Saratoga Springs, New York (Grand Union Hotel), and White Sulphur Springs, West Virginia (the Greenbrier). Other grand resort hotels built during the 1800s included the Hotel Del Coronado outside San Diego, California, the Ponce de Leon in St. Augustine, Florida, and the Broadmoor in Colorado Springs, Colorado.

Travelers who could not afford luxury accommodations usually were forced to stay at rundown roominghouses, which offered only minimal services and cleanliness. As rail transportation became affordable and more middle-class people began to travel, a new type of hostelry was needed to fill the gap between luxury hotels and roominghouses.

E. M. Statler recognized this demand and built the nation's first modern, commercial hotel in Buffalo, New York. When the Buffalo Statler opened in 1908, it offered many revolutionary conveniences: private baths, circulating ice water, full-length mirrors, overnight laundry, and free morning newspapers. Statler's slogan, "A room and a bath for a dollar and a half," put clean, comfortable transient accommodations within the reach of millions of Americans and increased the interest in travel among the middle class.

Prosperity, Decline, and Renewal

The economic prosperity of the 1920s produced one of the greatest hotel-building booms in America's history. Encouraged by rising occupancy rates, which exceeded 85% in 1920, hoteliers expanded existing properties and constructed hundreds of new and larger facilities. During this period the number of available hotel rooms in some cities doubled with the addition ot large convention properties. Chicago's 3,000-room Hotel Stevens (now the Chicago

Hilton) opened in 1927 and was the world's largest hotel for more than 35 years.

During the Roaring Twenties, hotel promoters set up shop in towns and cities throughout the United States and sold local residents on the idea that real estate was a sound and safe investment vehicle. Their sales pitch was not based on economic feasibility, but on civic pride and a chance to raise neighborhood or personal prestige. In some cases local merchants were promised patronage from hotel guests if they invested in the project.

Single Room Occupancy (SRO)

A single room occupancy is a multiple tenant building that houses one or two people in individual rooms (sometimes two rooms, or two rooms with a bathroom or half bathroom), or to the single room dwelling itself. SRO tenants typically share bathrooms and / or kitchens, while some SRO rooms may include kitchenettes, bathrooms, or half-baths. Although many are former hotels, SROs are primarily rented as a permanent residence.

The term originated in New York City, probably in the 1930s, but the institutions date back at least fifty years before the nickname was applied to them. SROs exist in many American cities, and are most common in larger cities. The terms single room occupancy and SRO are not used in British English. Related British terms include house in multiple occupation, hostel, bedsit or boarding house.

In many cases, the buildings themselves were formerly hotels in or near a city's central business district. Others are former single family homes. Many of these buildings were built in the late 19th and early 20th centuries, and reflect a high order of architectural style and craftsmanship.

A bedsit, also known as a bed-sitting room, is a form of rented accommodation common in Great Britain and Ireland consisting of a single room and shared bathroom; they are part of a legal category of dwellings referred to as Houses in multiple occupation.

Bedsits arose from the subdivision of larger dwellings into small low-cost accommodations at low conversion cost. In the UK a growing desire for personal independence after World War II led to a reduced demand for traditional boarding houses with communal dining.

Socially, bedsits are often occupied by young single people, students, those who are unable to purchase their own properties, or those who, for one reason or another, are of a transitory nature, because the living costs are comparatively cheaper than those afforded by private property.

Someone living in a different town from the one in which they work they may rent a bedsit at low cost to avoid driving many miles to and from work each day.

The American equivalents to a bedsit are single room occupancy (SRO) and rooming house. By comparison, a studio apartment (also known as a studio flat in the United Kingdom) is a one room apartment with a small adjoining kitchen and a private bathroom.

A bedsit can also be compared to a Soviet communal apartment, in which a common kitchen, bathroom, toilet, and telephone are shared by several families, each of which lives in a single room opening up onto a common hallway.

Option for Poor people

SROs are a viable housing option for poor people, students, single tenants, seasonal or other traveling workers, empty nester widows / widowers, or others who do not desire or require large dwellings or private domestic appliances. The smaller size and limited amenities in SROs generally makes them a more affordable housing option, especially in gentrifying neighborhoods or urban areas with high land values.

The rents of many disadvantaged tenants may be paid in full or in part by charitable, state and federal programs, giving incentive to landlords to accept such tenants. Some SRO buildings are renovated with the benefit of a tax abatement, with the condition that the rooms are rented to tenants with low incomes, and sometimes specific low income groups, such as homeless people, people with mental illness, people with AIDS, and so on.

Conditions

Depending on the sensibilities of the landlords and the quality of the properties, SRO conditions can range from squalor to something like an extended-stay hotel. Some have been run in dormitory fashion. Others have been "cage" hotels, in which a large room is split into many smaller ones with corrugated steel or sheetrock dividers, which do not reach the height of the original ceiling. To prevent tenants from climbing over the walls into each others' spaces, the tops of the rooms are covered in chicken wire, making the rooms look something like cages.

SROs Today

As the value of urban land has increased, it has become economical to renovate these properties and make them available once again to higher bidders. This would play a role in the displacement of people who once lived in them, and could be one reason for the visible increase in the population of homeless people in the streets of American cities since the early 1980s.

Recognizing that there is significant incentive for landlords to forcibly evict SRO tenants in gentrifying neighborhoods, some cities regulate the conversion of SROs to other use. In particular, if tenants testify that they have been harassed in any way, conversion can be delayed. In San Francisco, the city may take over particularly squalid SROs, and renovate them for the disadvantaged. Landlords who intend to convert SROs may try to convince their tenants to sign releases, which may require relocation by the landlord and / or compensating the tenant.

San Francisco similarly passed an SRO Hotel Conversion Ordinance in 1980, which restricts the conversion of SRO hotels to tourist use. SROs are prominent in the Tenderloin, Mission District and Chinatown communities. In 2001, San Francisco Supervisor Chris Daly sponsored legislation making it illegal for SRO landlords to charge "visitor fees" — a practice long run in order for hotel managers to get a "cut" on drug-dealing or prostitution activities in the building. After a rash of fires destroyed many SRO's in San Francisco and left nearly one thousand tenants homeless, a new program to reduce fire risk in SRO Hotels was initiated.

Apartment Hotel

An Apartment Hotel is also known as Aparthotel and Apart-hotel. It is a serviced apartment complex that uses a hotel-style booking system. It is similar to renting an apartment, but with no fixed contracts and occupants can 'check-out' whenever they wish.

The standard zoning definition, nationwide is:

"Apartment hotel means a building designed for or containing both apartments and individual guestrooms or rental units, under resident supervision, and which maintains an inner lobby through which all tenants must pass to gain access to apartments, rooms or units."

Apartment hotels are flexible types of accommodation; instead of the rigid format of a hotel room, an apartment hotel complex usually offers a complete fully fitted apartment. These complexes are usually custom built, and similar to a hotel complex containing a varied amount of apartments. The length of stay in these apartment hotels is varied with anywhere from a few days to months or even years. The people that stay in apartment hotels use them as a home away from home, therefore they are usually fitted with everything the average home would require.

Apartment hotels were first created in holiday destinations as accommodation for families that needed to 'live' in an apartment rather than 'stay' as they would in a hotel. The apartments would provide a 'holiday home' but generally be serviced. Later on these apartments evolved to be complete homes, allowing occupants to do everything they would at home, such as cleaning, washing and cooking.

Services and Facilities

Essentially the apartment hotel combines the flexibility of apartment living with the service of a hotel. Many of the apartments take advantage of prime locations with panoramic views of cities seen through wall to ceiling windows. Suites usually include high quality finishes, broadband connection & interactive TV, servicing and integrated kitchen and bathroom. High quality leather sofas in the living area and king size beds bring the hotel experience to a whole new level. Those are the luxuries, they also come with the basics: satellite or cable TV, washer, dryer, dishwasher, cooker, oven, fridge, freezer, sink, shower, bath, wardrobes, all the furnishings to be expected in a luxury home. Self contained apartments usually provide kitchen facilities that travel residents are able to cook foods at their convenience

Extended Stay Hotels

Extended stay hotels are a type of lodging with features unavailable at standard hotels. These features are intended to provide more home-like amenities. There are currently 27 extended stay chains in North America with at least 7 hotels, representing over 2,000 properties. There is substantial variation among extended stay hotels with respect to quality and the amenities that are available. Some of the economy chains attract clientele who use the hotels as semi-permanent lodging.

Extended-stay hotels typically have self-serve laundry facilities and offer discounts for extended stays, beginning at 5 or 7 days. They also have guestrooms (or "suites") with kitchens. The kitchens include at a minimum usually: a sink, a refrigerator (usually full size), a microwave oven, and a stovetop. Some kitchens also have dishwashers and conventional ovens.

Extended stay hotels are popular with business travelers on extended assignments, families in the midst of a relocation, and anyone else in need of temporary housing. Extended stay hotels are also used by travelers who appreciate the larger space a typical suite provides.

Residence Inn is credited with popularizing the "extended stay" concept. The chain was launched in 1975 in Wichita, Kansas by Jack DeBoer, and acquired by Marriott Corporation in 1987. As of April 2005, there were over 450 Residence Inn hotels in the United States, Canada and Mexico. Jack DeBoer has jumped back in the Extended Stay market developing a concept called Value Place.

Other upscale brands of extended-stay hotels, such as Staybridge Suites which is part of the InterContinental Hotels Group, have made this segment of the lodging industry one of the fastest-growing.

One of today's most popular long term lodging brands came from the merger of Extended Stay America and Homestead Hotels. Both these chains were already well established when they combined in 2004 to become Extended Stay Hotels with over 670 owned and operated properties nationwide.

Another worldwide hotel chain, Choice Hotels International, franchisor for name brands such as Comfort Inn, Comfort Suites, Sleep Inn and Quality Inn, entered the extended stay market with their MainStay Suites brand. They proceeded to acquire the Suburban Extended Stay hotel chain in 2005, making them a sizeable extended stay system with over 150 hotels open and under development.

In the United States, a popular low-budget extended stay chain is Intown Suites. The chain, which was founded in 1988, now has nearly 140 locations in 21 states, and is distinguised for offering weekly rates much lower than many other chain lodging companies in North America.

Since 1999, Motel 6, the popular U.S. budget lodging chain (owned by Accor Hotels) operates Studio 6, a chain of extended stay hotels that offer weekly rates and more amenities than the standard Motel 6 properties. Studio 6 provides a kitchen area in all its rooms, and allows pets. Studio 6 locations are in 18 U.S. states and Canada.

The extended stay concept is steadily spreading throughout Europe due to the increase in the number of travelers and business people visiting every year. The concept was organized by Belgium Housing and the chain of hotels covers 42 countries of Europe including all the major cities of the continent.

Growth and Development of Motel

A motel is a hotel designed for motorists, and usually has a parking area for motor vehicles. The term 'motel' in the United States can be considered somewhat outdated and few motel chains still exist (Motel 6 and Super8 are two of the most popular still in existence). Motels peaked in popularity in the 1960s with rising car travel.

In the year 2000, the American Hotel-Motel Association removed 'motel' from its name after considerable market research, and is now the American Hotel and Lodging Association. The association felt that the term 'lodging' more accurately reflects the large variety of different style hotels, including luxury and boutique hotels, suites, inns, budget, and extended stay hotels.

Entering dictionaries after World War II, the word motel, a portmanteau of *motor* and *hotel* or *motorists' hotel*, referred initially to a type of hotel consisting of a single building of connected rooms whose doors faced a parking lot and, in some circumstances, a common area; or a series of small cabins with common parking. As the United States highway system began to develop in the 1920s, long distance road journeys became more common and the need for inexpensive, easily accessible overnight accommodation sited close to the main routes, led to the growth of the motel concept.

Auto camps predated motels by a few years. Unlike motels, auto camps and tourist courts typically provided bed and breakfast or hotel-style service, usually with stand-alone cabins. After the introduction of the motel, auto camps continued in popularity through the Depression years and after World War II, their popularity finally starting to diminish with the construction of freeways and changes in consumer demands. Examples include the Rising Sun Auto Camp in Glacier National Park and Blue Bonnet Court in Texas. Such facilities were "mom-and-pop" facilities on the outskirts of a town that were as quirky as their owners. The 1935 City Directory for San Diego, CA lists "motel" type accommodations under Tourist Camps.

In contrast, though they remained "Mom and Pop" operations, motels quickly adopted a more homogenized appearance and were designed from the start to cater purely for motorists. The motel concept originated with the Motel Inn of San Luis Obispo, constructed in 1925 by Arthur Heineman. In conceiving of a name for his hotel Heineman abbreviated *motor hotel* to *mo-tel*.

Motels are typically constructed in an 'I'- or 'L'- or 'U - shaped layout that includes guest rooms, an attached manager's office, a small reception and, in some cases, a small diner. Post-war motels sought more visual distinction, often featuring eye-catching neon signs which employed themes from popular culture, ranging from Western imagery of cowboys and Indians to contemporary images of spaceships and atomic era iconography.

Motels differ from hotels in their location along highways, as opposed to the urban cores favored by hotels, and their orientation to the outside (in contrast to hotels whose doors typically face an interior hallway). Motels almost by definition include a parking lot, while older hotels were not usually built with automobile parking in mind.

With the 1952 introduction of Kemmons Wilson's Holiday Inn, the mom-and-pop motels of that era started to decline. The emergence of the interstate highway system, along with other factors, led to a blurring of the motel and the hotel, though family-owned motels with as few as five rooms may still be found, especially along older highways.

In the late 20th century, a majority of motels in the United States came under the ownership of people of Indian descent, particularly Gujaratis. Motels/hotels with low rates sometimes serve as housing for people who are not able to afford an apartment or have recently lost their home and need somewhere to stay until further arrangements are made. Motels catering to long-term stays often have kitchenettes. However, even though most of these establishments that were previously called motels may still look like motels, most are now called hotels, inns, lodges, etc.

10

THE GROWTH STRATEGIES OF TRAVEL INDUSTRY

An airline provides air transport services for passengers and/or freight. Airlines lease or own their aircraft with which to supply these services and may form partnerships or alliances with other airlines for mutual benefit. Generally, airline companies are recognized with an air operating certificate or license issued by a governmental aviation body.

Airlines vary from those with a single aircraft carrying mail or cargo, through full-service international airlines operating hundreds of aircraft. Airline services can be categorized as being intercontinental, intra-continental, domestic, regional, or international, and may be operated as scheduled services or charters.

Recession Growth Strategies

With forecasts predicting sustained economic and employment growth, improvements in capital markets and other favorable conditions, the nation's top restaurateurs, investors, lenders and advisors will gather in Los Angeles for the 15th Annual Restaurant Industry Conference to hear experts offer the latest research, insights – and inspiration.

Last year's Restaurant Industry Conference, sponsored by UCLA Extension, could very well be a bellwether moment for the $1.3 trillion industry and for the U.S. economy as a whole, organizers said.

"Restaurants lead out of a recession, so how they perform in 2011 could very well confirm the country is on the mend," said Anna Graves, conference chair and co-leader of the Restaurant, Food & Beverage Industry Group for Pillsbury Winthrop Shaw Pittman LLP. The conference takes place at the Hyatt Regency Century Plaza Hotel on Thursday, April 21.

The key for restaurant executives, Graves said, is to have the right approach to profitability and not take over-aggressive steps.

"The restaurant industry leaders who gather here in April recognize consumers continue to pinch pennies and running these businesses remains as challenging as ever. Yet, there is room for growth and having the right strategies in place will make all the difference for restaurants," she said.

The conference begins with two fact-filled sessions. Julia A. Stewart, chairman and CEO of DineEquity, will discuss the focus, fundamentals, and financial strategies which are necessary to successfully navigating out of a recession. Edward Leamer, a world-class economist and author of the highly acclaimed UCLA Anderson Business Forecast each year, will provide insights and direction on what 2011 will hold – and explain how restaurant operators might best prepare for it.

The early session will be completed with a "State of the Industry" panel discussion featuring Ron Paul, President, Technomic, Inc., and Nicole Miller Regan, Senior Research Analyst, Piper Jaffray, followed by breakout sessions discussing how to instill work ethics in younger workers and key issues in franchising.

The next session includes a panel offering the latest thinking about acquiring capital and insights into financial restructuring. The speakers are: Gene Baldwin, CRG

Partners; Kevin Burke, Managing Director, Trinity Capital; Bill Taves, CFO, Claim Jumper Restaurants; and H. G. ("Carey") Carrington Jr., CFO, Romano's Macaroni Grill. The session is moderated by Rod Guinn, Operating Partner of FocalPoint Partners LLC.

The final panel focuses on "emerging concepts," featuring CEOs of companies of companies that sustained significant growth during the recession and continue to outperform their competitors. These include Greg Dollarhyde, president & CEO of Zoë's Kitchen and Dave Prokupek, chairman & CEO of Smashburger. The session will be moderated by Wallace Doolin, Chairman, People Report & Black Box Intelligence.

The conference culminates with the presentation of the 2011 Innovation Award to José Andrés, chef and owner of the ThinkFoodGroup, which operates numerous restaurant concepts, including Jaleo, Café Atlántico, minibar by José Andrés, and Los Angeles' celebrated destination in the exclusive SLS Hotel, The Bazaar by José Andrés. Andres will accept the award from last year's winner, Kerry Kramp, President and CEO of Sizzler USA, Inc.

"José is credited with bringing the 'small plates' concept to the United States, considered one of the fathers of the molecular gastronomy movement, and internationally recognized as a culinary innovator," Graves said, adding that conference attendees will be treated to an informal and highly instructive one-on-one dialogue between Andrés and Kramp. "I think this discussion will be particularly interesting. While their concepts may be diametrically opposed, their extraordinary success in appealing to their particular guest base is shared."

Carlson reported a 12 percent increase of its system-wide sales in 2010 to USD 6.5 billion for its global hotel business. This announcement was made at the company's global hotel business conference in Washington, D.C.

"This strong sales performance is one of several key milestones that Carlson Hotels achieved in the first year of its Ambition 2015 strategy," said **Hubert** Joly, president and chief executive officer, Carlson. *"And, looking ahead, we have exciting plans to continue our momentum towards our Ambition 2015 objectives."*

Key accomplishments for Carlson Hotels in 2010 cover all of its strategic priorities.

Global Growth: Carlson signed 87 hotels and opened 66 hotels in 2010. The company's total number of rooms in operations and development crossed the 200,000 room threshold. And the number of hotels in operation reached 1,071 hotels at the end of 2010, despite the exit of 42 hotels that were non-compliant with system standards.

Brand Strategies:

- Over USD 500 million has been committed so far to the Radisson® strategy in North America and 80 percent of the existing Radisson portfolio in North America has committed to Property Improvement Plans aligned with the new global brand standards. Also, Radisson continued its rapid expansion with 41 new hotels signed in 2010, a 52 percent increase over 2009, including two new-build flagship properties in North America.
- Country Inns & Suites By Carlsonsm successfully launched its Be Our Guest Breakfast and continued the rollout of Generation 3 interior design installations in its hotels in North America.
- Park Inn continued its rapid growth with more than 110 hotels in operation and 50 hotels in development. It opened 20 hotels and had 23 signings, including three in North America.

Emerging Markets: The company continued its rapid expansion in key emerging markets which represented 60 percent of new signings in 2010, whereas they account for

18 percent of the hotels in operation. During the year, the company solidified its leadership positions in India, Russia / CIS and Africa in particular. Revenue Generation: Carlson's loyalty program reached 6.3 million members, a 24 percent increase over 2009.

Acquisitions: Carlson increased its ownership in The Rezidor Hotel Group to more than 50 percent, and the company acquired its key partner in India - RHW Hotel Management Services Ltd.

Looking ahead, Carlson Hotels, is focused on continuing the implementation of its Ambition 2015 strategy. Most notably:

- For Radisson, the main priorities are to implement the agreed upon Property Improvement Plans (more than 70 percent of them should be completed by 2013), and to continue the global expansion of the brand, with 44 openings expected in 2011, including the Radisson Blu Aqua Hotel, Chicago.
- Country Inns & Suites By Carlson will be the first midscale brand to introduce non-disposable tableware in its hotels in North America. The brand will also continue to progress its international expansion.
- Park Inn is being renamed Park Inn by Radissonsm. This bold, fresh midscale brand is positioned for growth in North America, Europe and key emerging markets.
- Revenue Generation will continue to be a key area of focus for Carlson in 2011. In particular, the company will launch its new loyalty program, Club Carlson, on March 31, 2011. Its investment in marketing and sales will increase in 2011 by 31 percent versus 2009, across e-commerce, sales, revenue optimization and distribution.

Early Development of Airline

Tony Jannus conducted the United State's first scheduled commercial airline flight on 1 January 1914 for the St. Petersburg-Tampa Airboat Line. The 23-minute flight traveled between St. Petersburg, Florida and Tampa, Florida, passing some 50 feet (15 m) above Tampa Bay in Jannus' Benoist XIV biplane flying boat. Chalk's International Airlines began service between Miami and Bimini in the Bahamas in February 1919. Based in Ft. Lauderdale, Chalk's claimed to be the oldest continuously operating airline in the United States until its closure in 2008.

Following World War I, the United States found itself swamped with aviators. Many decided to take their war-surplus aircraft on barnstorming campaigns, performing acrobatic maneuvers to woo crowds. In 1918, the United States Postal Service won the financial backing of Congress to begin experimenting with air mail service, initially using Curtiss Jenny aircraft that had been procured by the United States Army for reconnaissance missions on the Western Front.

Private operators were the first to fly the mail but due to numerous accidents the US Army was tasked with mail delivery. During the course of the Army's involvement they proved to be too unreliable and lost their air mail duties. By the mid-1920s, the Postal Service had developed its own air mail network, based on a transcontinental backbone between New York and San Francisco.

To supplant this service, they offered twelve contracts for spur routes to independent bidders. Some of the carriers that won these routes would, through time and mergers, evolve into Pan Am, Delta Air Lines, Braniff Airways, American Airlines, United Airlines (originally a division of Boeing), Trans World Airlines, Northwest Airlines, and Eastern Air Lines.

Service during the early 1920s was sporadic: most airlines at the time were focused on carrying bags of mail. In 1925, however, the Ford Motor Company bought out the

Stout Aircraft Company and began construction of the all-metal Ford Trimotor, which became the first successful American airliner. With a 12-passenger capacity, the Trimotor made passenger service potentially profitable. Air service was seen as a supplement to rail service in the American transportation network.

At the same time, Juan Trippe began a crusade to create an air network that would link America to the world, and he achieved this goal through his airline, Pan American World Airways, with a fleet of flying boats that linked Los Angeles to Shanghai and Boston to London. Pan Am and Northwest Airways (which began flights to Canada in the 1920s) were the only U.S. airlines to go international before the 1940s.

With the introduction of the Boeing 247 and Douglas DC-3 in the 1930s, the U.S. airline industry was generally profitable, even during the Great Depression. This trend continued until the beginning of World War II.

Development Since 1945

As governments met to set the standards and scope for an emergent civil air industry toward the end of the war, the U.S. took a position of maximum operating freedom; U.S. airline companies were not as hard-hit as European and the few Asian ones had been. This preference for "open skies" operating regimes continues, within limitations, to this day.

World War II, like World War I, brought new life to the airline industry. Many airlines in the Allied countries were flush from lease contracts to the military, and foresaw a future explosive demand for civil air transport, for both passengers and cargo. They were eager to invest in the newly emerging flagships of air travel such as the Boeing Stratocruiser, Lockheed Constellation, and Douglas DC-6. Most of these new aircraft were based on American bombers such as the B-29, which had spearheaded research into new technologies such as pressurization. Most offered increased efficiency from both added speed and greater payload.

In the 1950s, the De Havilland Comet, Boeing 707, Douglas DC-8, and Sud Aviation Caravelle became the first flagships of the Jet Age in the West, while the Soviet Union bloc had Tupolev Tu-104 and Tupolev Tu-124 in the fleets of state-owned carriers such as Czechoslovak ÈSA, Soviet Aeroflot and East-German Interflug. The Vickers Viscount and Lockheed L-188 Electra inaugurated turboprop transport.

The next big boost for the airlines would come in the 1970s, when the Boeing 747, McDonnell Douglas DC-10, and Lockheed L-1011 inaugurated widebody ("jumbo jet") service, which is still the standard in international travel. The Tupolev Tu-144 and its Western counterpart, Concorde, made supersonic travel a reality. Concorde first flew in 1969 and operated through 2003. In 1972, Airbus began producing Europe's most commercially successful line of airliners to date. The added efficiencies for these aircraft were often not in speed, but in passenger capacity, payload, and range. Airbus also features modern electronic cockpits that were common across their aircraft to enable pilots to fly multiple models with minimal cross-training.

1978's U.S. airline industry deregulation lowered barriers for new airlines just as a downturn occurred. New start-ups entered during the downturn, during which time they found aircraft and funding, contracted hangar and maintenance services, trained new employees, and recruited laid off staff from other airlines.

As the business cycle returned to normalcy, major airlines dominated their routes through aggressive pricing and additional capacity offerings, often swamping new startups. Only America West Airlines (which has since merged with US Airways) remained a significant survivor from this new entrant era, as dozens, even hundreds, have gone under.

In many ways, the biggest winner in the deregulated environment was the air passenger. Indeed, the U.S. witnessed an explosive growth in demand for air travel, as many millions who had never or rarely flown before became regular fliers, even joining frequent flyer loyalty programs and receiving free flights and other benefits from their flying. New services and higher frequencies meant that business fliers could fly to another city, do business, and return the same day, for almost any point in the country. Air travel's advantages put intercity bus lines under pressure, and most have withered away.

By the 1980s, almost half of the total flying in the world took place in the U.S., and today the domestic industry operates over 10,000 daily departures nationwide. Toward the end of the century, a new style of low cost airline emerged, offering a no-frills product at a lower price. Southwest Airlines, JetBlue, AirTran Airways, Skybus Airlines and other low-cost carriers began to represent a serious challenge to the so-called "legacy airlines", as did their low-cost counterparts in many other countries. Their commercial viability represented a serious competitive threat to the legacy carriers. However, of these, ATA and Skybus have since ceased operations.

Increasingly since 1978, US airlines have been reincorporated and spun off by newly created and interally led manangement companies, and thus becoming nothing more than operating units and subsidiaries with limited finanically decisive control. Among some of these holding companies and parent companies that are the relatively well known, are the UAL Corporation, along with the AMR Corporation, among a long list of airline holding companies sometime recognized worldwide.

Less recognized are the private equity firms which often seize managerial, financial, and board of directors control of distressed airline companies by temporarily investing large sums of capital in air carriers, so as to re-scheme an airlines assets into a profitable organization or liquidating an air carrier of their profitable and worthwhile routes and business operations.

Thus the last 50 years of the airline industry have varied from reasonably profitable, to devastatingly depressed. As the first major market to deregulate the industry in 1978, U.S. airlines have experienced more turbulence than almost any other country or region. Today, American Airlines is the only U.S. legacy carrier to survive bankruptcy-free.

The Airline Industry Bailout

Congress passed the Air Transportation Safety and System Stabilization Act (P.L. 107-42) in response to a severe liquidity crisis facing the already-troubled airline industry in the aftermath of the September 11th terrorist attacks. Congress sought to provide cash infusions to carriers for both the cost of the four-day federal shutdown of the airlines and the incremental losses incurred through December 31, 2001 as a result of the terrorist attacks. This resulted in the first government bailout of the 21st century.. Between 2000 and 2005 US airlines lost $30 billion with wage cuts of over $15 billion and 100,000 employees laid off..

In recognition of the essential national economic role of a healthy aviation system, Congress authorized partial compensation of up to $5 billion in cash subject to review by the Department of Transportation and up to $10 billion in loan guarantees subject to review by a newly created Air Transportation Stabilization Board (ATSB). The applications to DOT for reimbursements were subjected to rigorous multi-year reviews not only by DOT program personnel but also by the Government Accountability Office and the DOT Inspector General.

Ultimately, the federal government provided $4.6 billion in one-time, subject-to-income-tax cash payments to 427 U.S. air carriers, with no provision for repayment, essentially a gift from the taxpayers. (Passenger carriers operating scheduled service received approximately $4 billion, subject to tax.) In addition, the ATSB approved loan guarantees to six airlines totaling approximately $1.6 billion.

Data from the Treasury Department show that the government recouped the $1.6 billion and a profit of $339 million from the fees, interest and purchase of discounted airline stock associated with loan guarantees.

European Airline Industry

The first countries in Europe to embrace air transport were Austria, Belgium, Finland, France, Germany, the Netherlands and the United Kingdom. Austria initiated the first regularly scheduled airmail service on March 31, 1918 in the midst of World War I. The route provided airmail service spanning Vienna to Krakow (now in Poland) to Lviv (now in Ukraine), as was often also extended to Kiev and Odessa.

KLM, the oldest carrier still operating under its original name, was founded in 1919. The first flight (operated on behalf of KLM by Aircraft Transport and Travel) transported two English passengers to Schiphol, Amsterdam from London in 1920. Like other major European airlines of the time, KLM's early growth depended heavily on the needs to service links with far-flung colonial possessions (Dutch Indies). It is only after the loss of the Dutch Empire that KLM found itself based at a small country with few potential passengers, depending heavily on transfer traffic, and was one of the first to introduce the hub-system to facilitate easy connections.

France began an air mail service to Morocco in 1919 that was bought out in 1927, renamed Aéropostale, and injected with capital to become a major international carrier. In 1933, Aéropostale went bankrupt, was nationalized and merged with several other airlines into what became Air France.

In Finland, the charter establishing Aero O/Y (now Finnair) was signed in the city of Helsinki on September 12, 1923. Junkers F 13 D-335 became the first aircraft of the company, when Aero took delivery of it on March 14, 1924.

The first flight was between Helsinki and Tallinn, capital of Estonia, and it took place on March 20, 1924, one week later.

Germany's Lufthansa began in 1926. Lufthansa, unlike most other airlines at the time, became a major investor in airlines outside of Europe, providing capital to Varig and Avianca. German airliners built by Junkers, Dornier, and Fokker were the most advanced in the world at the time. In 1931, the airship Graf Zeppelin began offering regular scheduled passenger service between Germany and South America, usually every two weeks, which continued until 1937. In 1936, the airship Hindenburg entered passenger service and successfully crossed the Atlantic 36 times before crashing at Lakehurst, New Jersey on May 6, 1937.

The British company Aircraft Transport and Travel commenced a London to Paris service on August 25, 1919, this was the world's first regular international flight. The United Kingdom's flag carrier during this period was Imperial Airways, which became BOAC (British Overseas Airways Co.) in 1939. Imperial Airways used huge Handley-Page biplanes for routes between London, the Middle East, and India: images of Imperial aircraft in the middle of the Rub'al Khali, being maintained by Bedouins, are among the most famous pictures from the heyday of the British Empire.

In Soviet Union the Chief Administration of the Civil Air Fleet was established in 1921. One of its first acts was to help found Deutsch-Russische Luftverkehrs A.G. (Deruluft), a German-Russian joint venture to provide air transport from Russia to the West. Domestic air service began around the same time, when Dobrolyot started operations on 15 July 1923 between Moscow and Nizhni Novgorod. Since 1932 all operations had been carried under the name Aeroflot. By the end of the 1930s Aeroflot had become the world's largest airline, employing more than 4,000 pilots and 60,000 other service personnel and operating around 3,000 aircraft (of which 75% were considered obsolete by its own standards). During the Soviet era Aeroflot was synonymous with

Russian civil aviation, as it was the only air carrier. It became the first airline in the world to operate sustained regular jet services on 15 September 1956 with the Tupolev Tu-104.

Deregulation

Deregulation of the European Union airspace in the early 1990s has had substantial effect on structure of the industry there. The shift towards 'budget' airlines on shorter routes has been significant. Airlines such as EasyJet and Ryanair have grown at the expense of the traditional national airlines.

There has also been a trend for these national airlines themselves to be privatised such as has occurred for Aer Lingus and British Airways. Other national airlines, including Italy's Alitalia, have suffered - particularly with the rapid increase of oil prices in early 2008.

Asian Airline Industry

Although Philippine Airlines (PAL) was officially founded on February 26, 1941, its license to operate as an airliner was derived from merged Philippine Aerial Taxi Company (PATCO) established by mining magnate Emmanuel N. Bachrach on December 3, 1930, making it Asia's oldest scheduled carrier still in operation.Commercial air service commenced three weeks later from Manila to Baguio, making it Asia's first airline route. Bachrach's death in 1937 paved the way for its eventual merger with Philippine Airlines in March 1941 and made it Asia's oldest airline.

It is also the oldest airline in Asia still operating under its current name. Bachrach's majority share in PATCO was bought by beer magnate Andres R. Soriano in 1939 upon the advice of General Douglas McArthur and later merged with newly formed Philippine Airlines with PAL as the surviving entity. Soriano has controlling interest in both airlines before the merger. PAL restarted service on March 15, 1941 with a single Beech Model 18 NPC-54 aircraft, which started its daily services between Manila (from Nielson Field) and Baguio, later to expand with larger aircraft such as the DC-3 and Vickers Viscount.

India was also one of the first countries to embrace civil aviation. One of the first West Asian airline companies was Air India, which had its beginning as Tata Airlines in 1932, a division of Tata Sons Ltd. (now Tata Group). The airline was founded by India's leading industrialist, JRD Tata. On October 15, 1932, J. R. D. Tata himself flew a single engined De Havilland Puss Moth carrying air mail (postal mail of Imperial Airways) from Karachi to Mumbai via Ahmedabad. The aircraft continued to Madras via Bellary piloted by Royal Air Force pilot Nevill Vintcent . Tata Airlines was also one of the world's first major airlines which began its operations without any support from the Government.

With the outbreak of World War II, the airline presence in Asia came to a relative halt, with many new flag carriers donating their aircraft for military aid and other uses. Following the end of the war in 1945, regular commercial service was restored in India and Tata Airlines became a public limited company on July 29, 1946 under the name Air India. After the independence of India, 49% of the airline was acquired by the Government of India. In return, the airline was granted status to operate international services from India as the designated flag carrier under the name Air India International.

On July 31, 1946, a chartered Philippine Airlines (PAL) DC-4 ferried 40 American servicemen to Oakland, California from Nielson Airport in Makati City with stops in Guam, Wake Island, Johnston Atoll and Honolulu, Hawaii, making PAL the first Asian airline to cross the Pacific Ocean. A regular service between Manila and San Francisco was started in December. It was during this year that the airline was designated as the flag carrier of Philippines.

During the era of decolonization, newly-born Asian countries started to embrace air transport. Among the first Asian carriers during the era were Cathay Pacific of Hong Kong (founded in September 1946), Orient Airways (later Pakistan International Airlines; founded in October 1946), Malayan Airlines (later Singapore and Malaysia Airlines; founded in 1947), El Al in Israel in 1948, Garuda Indonesia in 1949, Japan Airlines in 1951, and Korean Air in 1962.

Latin American Airline Industry

Among the first countries to have regular airlines in Latin America were Colombia with Avianca, Brazil with Varig, Chile with LAN Chile (today LAN Airlines), Dominican Republic with Dominicana de Aviación, Mexico with Mexicana de Aviación, and TACA as a brand of several airlines of Central American countries (Honduras, El Salvador, Costa Rica, Guatemala and Nicaragua). All the previous airlines started regular operations before World War II.

The air travel market has evolved rapidly over recent years in Latin America. Some industry estimations over 2000 new aircraft will begin service over the next five years in this region. These airlines serve domestic flights within their countries, as well as connections within Latin America and also overseas flights to North America, Europe, Australia, Africa and Asia.

Just three airlines: LAN (Latin American Networks), Oceanair and TAM Airlines have international subsidiaries with Chile as the central operation along with Peru, Ecuador, Argentina and some operations in the Dominican Republic and TAM with TAM Mercosur have a base in Asuncion, Paraguay. Avianca have the control of Oceanair, VIP Airlines and also have an estrategic alliance with TACA. The three main hubs in Latin America are Mexico City in Mexico, São Paulo in Brazil and Santiago in Chile.

National

Many countries have national airlines that the government owns and operates. Fully private airlines are subject to a great deal of government regulation for economic, political, and safety concerns. For instance, governments often intervene to halt airline labor actions in order to protect the free flow of people, communications, and goods between different regions without compromising safety.

The United States, Australia, and to a lesser extent Brazil, Mexico, India, the United Kingdom and Japan have "deregulated" their airlines. In the past, these governments dictated airfares, route networks, and other operational requirements for each airline. Since deregulation, airlines have been largely free to negotiate their own operating arrangements with different airports, enter and exit routes easily, and to levy airfares and supply flights according to market demand.

The entry barriers for new airlines are lower in a deregulated market, and so the U.S. has seen hundreds of airlines start up (sometimes for only a brief operating period). This has produced far greater competition than before deregulation in most markets, and average fares tend to drop 20% or more. The added competition, together with pricing freedom, means that new entrants often take market share with highly reduced rates that, to a limited degree, full service airlines must match. This is a major constraint on profitability for established carriers, which tend to have a higher cost base.

As a result, profitability in a deregulated market is uneven for most airlines. These forces have caused some major airlines to go out of business, in addition to most of the poorly established new entrants.

BIBLIOGRAPHY

- Associated Press. 1994. Pigs Dig In To Help Recycle Trash. New York TImes. February 20: p. 49 Col 1.
- Brown, K. 1993. Source Reduction Now: How to Implement a Source Reduction Program in Your Organization. Minnesota Office of Waste Management. St. Paul, Minnesota.
- Cornell Hotel and Restaurant Quarterly. 1993. The Three R's: Reduce, Reuse, Recycle. Cornell Hotel and Restaurant Quarterly. October: 18.
- Egan, K. 1996. McDonald's Continues Work To Reduce Waste. Waste Age's Recycling Times. May 14: 10.
- Egan, K. 1996. Recycling, Waste Reduction Becoming a Larger Part of the Hotel Industry. Waste Age's Recycling Times. May 14: 13.
- Ferris, D. and C. Shanklin, etal. 1994. Solid Waste Management in Foodservice. Food Technology. March: 110-115.
- Florida Energy Extension Service. 1996. Recycling in Hotels and Motels (video). University of Florida. Gainesville, Florida.
- Foster, D. 1995. Enthusiasm For Recycling Finally Translates Into Big Business. Las Vegas Review Journal. May 2: 10B.

• Restaurant Management Insider. 1992. The Forty-Five best Insider Profit Tips for Restaurateurs. Walker Communications Incorporated. New York.

• River City Resource Group. 1996. Green Plate Restaurant Recycling Guide. River City Resource Group. Portland, Oregon.

• Saunders. T. 1993. The Bottom Line of Green is Black: Strategies for Creating a Profitable and Environmentally Sound Business. Harper. San Francisco, California.

• Saunders. T. 1995. Employees Drive Hotel's Waste Reduction Success: Waste Reduction Tips. Environmental Newsletter. May/June.

• Swartz, J. 1988. Turning trash Into Hard Cash. Newsweek. March 14: 36-37.

• Teitenberg, T. 1992. Environmental and Natural Resource Economics. Harper Collins Publishers Inc. New York.

• Wagner, M. 1995. Food Waste Recovery: Just Another Way to Reduce Waste. Resource Recycling. October: 75-77.

• Washington Retail Association. 1992. Preferred Packaging Procurement Guidelines. Washington Retail Association. Olympia, Washington.

• Watkins, E. 1994. Do Guests Want Green Hotels? Lodging Hospitality. April: 70-72.

• Wendy's Restaurant. 1996. Recycling at Wendy's. Corporate Pamphlet.

• Westerman, M. 1991. Restaurants Recycle. Resource Recycling. January: 78-83.

• Whiffen, H. 1992. Recycling x Energy Savings=Earth's Survival. Florida Hotel and Motel Journal. July: 37.

• White, P. 1983. The Fascinating World of Trash. National Geographic Magazine. April: 425-457.

INDEX